THE LAWBOOK

Everyday law
from
Allianz Legal Protection

Published by
Jordan & Sons Limited
21 St. Thomas Street, Bristol BS1 6JS

ISBN 0 85308 094 1

DISCLAIMER

While the contents of this book are believed to be correct, they should
not be taken as sufficiently full or accurate to apply to any particular situation –
advice should be taken in all cases. Names, addresses and telephone numbers
contained in the 'Contact Points' were correct at the time of going to press,
but may have subsequently changed.

Typeset by Profile Filmsetters Ltd, Salisbury

Printed in Great Britain by The Eastern Press Ltd., London and Reading

Preface

Everyone whether at home, work or play, has daily contact with the laws of the country, usually without knowing it. Often you want to know your legal position either to enable you to exercise your legal rights or to know your legal obligations.

Although written Codes of Practice exist in employment and there is a Highway Code for road users, to date there hasn't been a concise portable ready reference guide to this huge subject. All the while however, everyone knows that ignorance of the law gives us no defence in court and that it is usually expensive to learn about your legal rights from a professional advisor.

It is my aim through my work in the legal protection insurance industry to make the law both more accessible and less expensive. Hopefully this guide goes some way to achieving the first objective, and of course it won't surprise you to learn that I see the wholesale adoption in this country (as has already been the case in mainland Europe) of legal fees insurance as a means to achieve the second objective.

Since lawyers need large libraries full of books, it is hardly surprising that this short volume is restricted to a brief overview of matters which arise fairly frequently. It does not pretend to cover all aspects of the law and those that are covered are often dealt with in a general rather than a detailed way. For these reasons it will not provide the whole answer to many problems – each of which has its own special circumstances and characteristics; nor is it an alternative to obtaining the professional advice of a lawyer. However, it should answer many of your more usual queries and it could also alert you to danger signs where the early advice of a lawyer – on the stitch-in-time principle – will pay dividends. Of course, for that diminishing number of you who can obtain legal aid, or the growing number legally insured, that advice and any resulting court action need not cost you anything.

Each chapter ends with a list of useful contact points, many with detailed addresses and telephone numbers. The purpose of this is to give the guide added usefulness because you may be able to obtain just the assistance you need from a specialist, pressure or other group without having to go to the law. Whilst these groups, their addresses and telephone numbers were accurate at the time of going to press, you will appreciate that such information may change without our knowledge. A glossary of some legal words and phrases, including those in use in Scotland, is also included at the end of the book.

It is our aim to constantly up-date this book and perhaps to extend it into other areas not covered in this first edition, and for both reasons readers' comments are welcomed. The law contained in this edition covers England and Wales, Scotland and Northern Ireland, and is stated as at November 1987.

On the legal horizon can already be seen proposals for dramatic changes in legal procedures and the structure of the courts, heralded by The Lord Chancellor's Civil Justice Review. What is certain, however, is that with the passing of the Access to Personal Files Act and the right, from 11 November 1987, to inspect data under the Data Protection Act, information which might before have been inaccessible can no longer be kept from those whom it directly concerns – a thoroughly healthy sign in a democracy such as ours.

John C Long, Solicitor,
Managing Director,
Allianz Legal Protection

November 1987

Introduction

Allianz was founded in 1890 and has become Europe's largest insurance group. Its head office is in Munich. In 1973 Allianz International Insurance Company Limited was incorporated in London and in January 1986 Allianz acquired Cornhill Insurance Group. One month later it took a key step in expanding the Allianz Group legal protection network into the UK, when it acquired a controlling interest in Allianz Legal Protection.

Legal protection insurance originated in France at the beginning of this century and its establishment in Europe followed the growth in the use of motor transport, as the early policies were vehicle related. Since the early 1920's demand has grown rapidly, especially in Germany, although such insurance was, by laws dating from the Middle Ages, illegal in the UK until the Criminal Law Act 1967. It was only in 1974 that the first legal protection policies were launched by a Lloyd's of London insurance broker.

Legal protection insurance provides cover to pay legal fees and associated expenses arising from the pursuit or defence of the legal rights of individuals or businesses. Criminal legal protection is available to defend prosecutions, but fines, penalties or prosecution costs are not covered because to do so would offend against public policy. However, legal protection insurance will, in civil cases, also pay any costs awarded against the insured should the claim be unsuccessful.

Authorship of the Allianz Lawbook is rightly attributed to the Claims Department of Allianz Legal Protection who would like to acknowledge with thanks the very valuable assistance given to them by their respective colleagues and others, including Stuart Cliffe FCII, James Collett solicitor, Heather Debeir solicitor, Eileen Gardiner BA, Victoria Kaye, Sarah McMurchie solicitor, Allan Truman ACII, Robert Spicer and Richard Smith barristers at law, and for the Scottish variations, Iain McLean solicitor, and for Northern Ireland, Ernest Telford and Desmond Doris solicitors. Dr C A Collett MBBS, MRCS, LRCP, advised on the medical aspects of Chapter 4.

Contents

Preface   **i**

Introduction   **iii**

Contents   **v**

1. Law and Order   **1**

1.1	Sources of Law	1
1.2	The Hierarchy of the Courts	1
	The European connection	1
	The judiciary	2
	Northern Ireland	4
	Scotland	4
1.3	The Legal Profession	8
	Solicitors	8
	Barristers	9
1.4	Legal Aid	9
	Types of legal aid	10
	Legal advice and assistance	10
	Assistance by way of representation	12
	Civil legal aid	12
	Criminal legal aid	13
1.5	Legal Expenses Insurance	14
1.6	The Police	15
	Police hierarchy	15
	Police powers	16
	Powers to stop and search	16
	Power of arrest	17
	Power of detention	18
	Charging	19
	Habeas corpus	20
	Entry and search of premises	20
	Search with or without warrant	20

Contents

Searching after arrest 21
Seizure 21
Search of persons 21
The right to legal advice and assistance 22
Complaints against the police 22
1.7 Sentencing 23
1.8 The Crown Prosecution Service 25
1.9 Bail 26
1.10 Contact Points 26

2. The Road User 27

2.1 Buying a Car From a Dealer 27
How to Complain 28
Your legal remedies 29
2.2 Buying from a Private Individual 29
2.3 Finance 30
HP agreements 30
Default and repossession 30
Conditional sale agreement 31
Credit sale agreement 31
Do's and don'ts on buying cars 31
2.4 Selling a Car 31
2.5 Auction Sales 32
2.6 Repairs and Servicing 32
Checklist: repair and servicing 33
How to complain 33
2.7 Documentation 34
2.8 Taking your Car Abroad 35
2.9 Car Hire 36
2.10 Car Parking 37
2.11 Road Traffic Offences 37
Seat belts 38
General maintenance 38
Causing death by reckless driving 39
Reckless driving 39
Careless and inconsiderate driving 39
Failing to stop after an accident and give particulars or report an
accident 39
Driving without a licence 40
Driving with uncorrected defective eyesight or refusing to submit to
a sight test 40
Using vehicle without minimum legal insurance cover 40

2.12 Drink and Driving   40
      Breath tests   41
      Driving or attempting to drive when unfit through drink or drugs   42
      Being in charge of a motor vehicle when unfit through drink or drugs 42
      *Driving or attempting to drive with excess alcohol in breath, blood
          or urine*   42
      *Being in charge of a motor vehicle with excess alcohol in breath,
          blood or urine*   42
      Failing to provide a specimen of breath for a breath test   43
      Failing to provide a specimen for analysis or laboratory test   43
2.13 Contact Points   43

3. The Home   **47**

3.1   Buying and Selling a Home   47
      Preliminary matters   47
      Deposits   48
      The contract   48
      Exchange and completion   49
      Conveyancing costs   49
3.2   Guarantees   50
      National House Building Council   50
      Damp and timber treatment   50
3.3   Joint Ownership   51
3.4   Renting Property   51
      Rent Acts   51
      Tenancy agreements   52
      Landlord's responsibilities   53
      Tenant's responsibilities   53
      Shorthold tenancies   53
      Fair rents   54
      Letting your home temporarily   54
      Letting your retirement home   55
      Sub-letting   55
      Sharing rented accommodation   55
      Notice   55
      Insurance   56
3.5   Home Improvements   56
      Finance   56
      Legal Aspects   57
      Planning permission and building regulations   57
3.6   Offences Relating to Property   58
      Trespass   58

Contents

	Rights of way	59
	Children	60
	Squatting	60
	Nuisance	60
3.7	Occupier's Liability	61
3.8	Removals	61
3.9	Contact Points	61

4. The Family		**69**
4.1	Engagement	69
4.2	Marriage	69
	Church marriages	70
	Civil marriages	71
	Marital rights and obligations	71
	Finance	71
	Property	72
4.3	Bigamy and Polygamy	72
4.4	Cohabitation	72
4.5	Domestic Violence	73
4.6	Termination of Marriage	74
	Divorce	74
	Divorce procedure	75
	Separation	76
	Annulment	76
	Maintenance payments	77
	Conciliation	77
	Presumption of death	78
	Custody of children	78
	Child abduction	78
4.7	Children	79
	Birth	79
	Contraception	80
	Abortion	80
	Illegitimacy	80
	Adoption	80
	Custodianship	81
	Fostering	81
	Wardship	82
	Parental obligations towards children	82
	How the law affects children	82
	Juvenile crime	83

	Minimum age-limits	83
	Child abuse	85
4.8	Animals	86
4.9	Medical Matters	86
	Hospital	87
	Consent	87
	Discharge from hospital	87
	Complaints against a hospital	88
	Complaints against a GP	88
4.10	Mental Health	89
	The Court of Protection	89
	Power of attorney	89
4.11	Death	90
	Post mortem	90
	Inquest (in Scotland, fatal accident inquiry)	91
	Human remains	92
	Funerals	92
4.12	Wills, Probate and Intestacy	93
	Challenging a will	93
	The effect of marriage and divorce on the will	94
	Obtaining a grant	94
	Intestacy	95
	Personal representatives (executors or administrators)	95
	Inheritance Tax	96
4.13	Contact Points	96

5. Consumer Affairs **107**

5.1	Buying Goods	107
	Rights and remedies	107
5.2	Buying Services	108
5.3	Unfair Contract Terms Act	109
5.4	Private Sales	109
5.5	Buying at Auctions	110
5.6	Doorstep Sales	110
5.7	Deposits	110
5.8	Unsolicited Goods and Services	110
5.9	Buying by Post	111
5.10	Consumer Complaints	111
	Arbitration	112
	Going to court	112
	Remedies	113
	Who can help ?	113

Contents

5.11	Banking	114
5.12	Credit	115
	Credit cards	115
	Hire purchase and credit sales	116
	Bank overdrafts and loans	117
5.13	Consumer Safety	117
	Safety standards	117
	Food	118
	Product liability	119
5.14	Eating Out	119
5.15	Advertising	120
5.16	Holidays	120
	Booking	121
	Foreign Laws	121
	Customs	122
5.17	Public Houses	122
5.18	Firearms	123
5.19	Contact Points	124

6.	**Employment Matters**	**129**
6.1	Contract of Employment	129
	Implied terms	130
	Wages	130
	Sickness	131
	Hours of work	131
	Termination of the contract of employment	131
	References	132
6.2	Maternity Rights	132
6.3	Disciplinary Rules and Procedures	133
6.4	Unfair Dismissal	133
	Industrial tribunals	134
	Remedies for unfair dismissal	135
6.5	Redundancy	135
6.6	Wrongful Dismissal	136
6.7	Equal Pay	136
6.8	Trade Unions	137
6.9	The Advisory Conciliation and Arbitration Service (ACAS)	137
6.10	Wages Councils	138
6.11	Industrial Safety	138
6.12	Contact Points	139

7. Accidents   143

7.1 Negligence   143
     Claiming damages   144
     Contributory negligence   145
     Time limits   145
     'Strict liability'   145
7.2 Accidents   146
     Road accidents   146
     Accidents at work   146
     Accidents at school   148
     Accidents at home   148
     Sporting accidents   149
7.3 Criminal Injuries   149
7.4 Contact Points   150

8. Insurance   151

8.1 The Policy   151
8.2 Brokers   151
8.3 Insurance Companies   152
8.4 Claims   152
8.5 Types of Insurance   152
     Personal accident and sickness insurance   153
     Permanent health insurance   153
     Life assurance   153
     Medical insurance   154
     Pensions   154
     Motor insurance   154
     Home insurance   157
     Occupier's liability   158
     Holiday homes and retirement homes   158
8.6 Contact Points   158

Glossary   161

Index   171

1. Law and Order

This introductory chapter looks at the structure of the legal system in England and Wales, Scotland and Northern Ireland – the people involved and the way justice is administered. We look in turn at the courts themselves, the legal aid system, and the police and criminal justice.

1.1 Sources of Law

Unlike elsewhere in the EEC, the UK does not have a written constitution; nor do we have a Bill or Act of Rights. Our law is based upon case law and statute law. Case law has evolved from decisions made by judges in the courts of law, which, until 'overturned' in higher courts or by an Act of Parliament, create 'precedents' or binding decisions which lower courts must follow.

Statute law is passed by both Houses of Parliament, and comes into force when it receives the Royal Assent from the Queen – a formality these days as the Sovereign takes no part in the legislative process. It is, however, left to the courts to interpret the enacted law.

Very occasionally local custom and practice may be relied upon to prove the existence of a legal right.

1.2 The Hierarchy of Courts

The English court structure is divided into criminal and civil jurisdiction, although some courts hear both types of case (see the diagrams on pages 5–8).

The European connection

Britain has been a member of the European Economic Community since 1973, and our legal system is now fully integrated into that of Europe.

EEC law stems from a number of treaties which confer powers on the four principal institutions of the Community. These are:

- The Council
- The Community
- The Assembly
- The Court of Justice

Under the EEC treaties , legislation is made by The Council, based on proposals from the Commission on which all member states are represented. It is issued in the form of :

(a) *Regulations,* which are directly and immediately binding on member states;

(b) *Directives,* which are binding as to the end result which is to be achieved although each member state may select the appropriate legislative method of implementation;

(c) *Decisions,* which are binding on those to whom they are addressed, whether they be a member state, corporation or individual.

The Court of Justice interprets and implements European Community law, and is composed of one judge for each member state.

European Community law operates in parallel with English law, but in any case of conflict, the European Community law must prevail. Cases heard by the court are reported in published reports in each of the official languages of the Community. Cases from the English legal system may be referred to the European Court of Justice with the permission of the House of Lords. The European Court is now the ultimate Court of Appeal within our system, and can only be used after the English appeal system has been exhausted. Decisions made by the court are, however, only persuasive and the English courts to which they apply are not bound to follow the decision.

The judiciary

There is an order of precedence for the judiciary and officers of the court, starting with the most senior and working down:

The Lord Chancellor is appointed by the Crown on the advice of the Prime Minister of the day, and is the highest ranking member of the judiciary. He is a member of the Cabinet, the speaker of the House of Lords, and the presiding judge at judicial proceedings on appeal.

Lords of Appeal are senior members of the judiciary and are usually appointed from the Courts of Appeal. They hear and decide cases in the House of Lords.

The Lord Chief Justice is appointed by the Monarch on the recommendation of the Prime Minister, and presides over the Queen's Bench Division of the High Court and the Criminal Division of the Court of Appeal.

The Queen's Bench Division encompasses the Admiralty Court and the Commercial Court. There are also Divisional Courts which comprise at least two judges of the High Court to deal mainly with appeals and supervisory work.

The Master of the Rolls is a member of the High Court and because of his position, is also a member of the Court of Appeal, presiding over the Civil Division. He also has responsibility for the 'Roll' of solicitors.

The President of the Family Division is in charge of that Division of the High Court.

The Vice Chancellor is responsible for the Chancery Division of the High Court, which also includes the Patents Court.

Lords Justices of Appeal are judges who sit in the Court of Appeal, appointed by the Monarch from judges in the High Court, or barristers of at least 15 years standing.

Judges of the High Court are those who practice in that Court's three divisions of Chancery, Queen's Bench and Family.

The Attorney-General is the chief law officer of the Crown, and head of English barristers, or 'the bar'. He can both represent the interests of the Crown in legal proceedings and conduct prosecutions on the Crown's behalf.

The Solicitor General is the Deputy to the Attorney-General, a law officer of the Crown, and is usually a member of the House of Commons, his role being largely advisory.

Circuit judges are appointed by the Queen on the recommendation of the Lord Chancellor, to try criminal cases in the Crown Court, and to sit as county court judges for civil matters. They must be barristers or solicitors of at least 10 years standing.

Queen's or *King's* (as appropriate) *Counsel* are senior barristers appointed on the recommendation of the Lord Chancellor, who wear a silk gown and may appear in any case.

Magistrates are usually lay people, who have been nominated perhaps by their local political party, a voluntary organisation in which they are active, or a trade union. However, there are a number of salaried magistrates who serve mainly in the London area, known as 'stipendiary magistrates'. This system also operates in Northern Ireland, where the magistrates are known as 'resident magistrates'. Stipendiary magistrates operate also in Glasgow.

Most criminal cases are heard initially by magistrates, who have the power to impose prison sentences of up to six months, depending upon the type of offence. If they are presented with a case which they feel should receive a harsher sentence than they are empowered to give, then they may commit the case to the Crown Court for sentencing. Magistrates also issue warrants for search and arrest to the police, and deal with other civil matters such as adoption, maintenance and affiliation proceedings.

Northern Ireland

In Northern Ireland, the highest judicial officer is the Lord Chief Justice who presides over all civil and criminal matters in the High Court. In addition he is the Lord Chancellor's Representative in Northern Ireland and is responsible for all judicial appointments in the province. There is no equivalent to the Master of the Rolls or the Vice Chancellor.

Scotland

As in England, the main function of a judge is to ensure that rules of procedure and evidence are followed and that justice is done and seen to be done. Again, different judges preside over different courts. Starting with the lowest court, the structure is:

The district court (criminal matters only), presided over by a legally qualified stipendiary magistrate (Glasgow only), or by a lay magistrate with a qualified assessor elsewhere.

The sheriff court, presided over by a sheriff, either alone (civil matters) or with a jury (serious criminal matters); or by the Sheriff Principal to hear civil appeals from the sheriff court.

The Court of Session, which hears appeals from the sheriff court and appeals against the decisions of a Sheriff Principal. The Court of Session can also hear cases in its own right, and historically was the only court which could hear divorce actions. The law in this matter has changed, and it is now possible to bring an action of divorce in the sheriff court. Where there is a major sum of money involved, or the question is one of great complexity, however, there remains a tendency to raise the action in the Court of Session.

The High Court of Justiciary. This is the highest court in Scotland with reference to criminal matters. It will hear appeals from the district and sheriff courts, and it will also hear the most serious criminal cases.

Courts in England and Wales

Superior courts in England and Wales

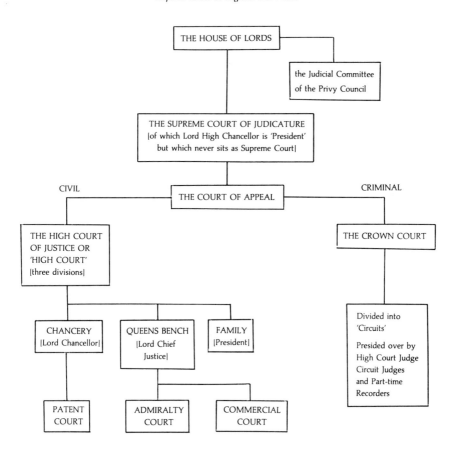

THE HOUSE OF LORDS

the Judicial Committee of the Privy Council

THE SUPREME COURT OF JUDICATURE
|of which Lord High Chancellor is 'President' but which never sits as Supreme Court|

CIVIL   THE COURT OF APPEAL   CRIMINAL

THE HIGH COURT OF JUSTICE OR 'HIGH COURT' |three divisions|

THE CROWN COURT

CHANCERY |Lord Chancellor|

QUEENS BENCH |Lord Chief Justice|

FAMILY |President|

Divided into 'Circuits'

Presided over by High Court Judge Circuit Judges and Part-time Recorders

PATENT COURT

ADMIRALTY COURT

COMMERCIAL COURT

1.2 The hierarchy of courts

Inferior courts in England and Wales

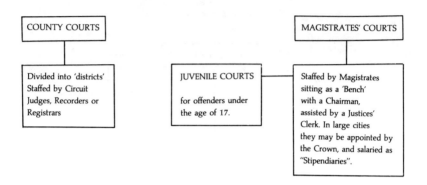

COUNTY COURTS		MAGISTRATES' COURTS
Divided into 'districts' Staffed by Circuit Judges, Recorders or Registrars	JUVENILE COURTS for offenders under the age of 17.	Staffed by Magistrates sitting as a 'Bench' with a Chairman, assisted by a Justices' Clerk. In large cities they may be appointed by the Crown, and salaried as "Stipendiaries".

Special courts and tribunals

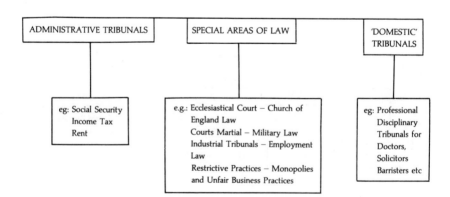

ADMINISTRATIVE TRIBUNALS	SPECIAL AREAS OF LAW	'DOMESTIC' TRIBUNALS

eg: Social Security
    Income Tax
    Rent
	e.g.: Ecclesiastical Court – Church of England Law
	Courts Martial – Military Law
	Industrial Tribunals – Employment Law
	Restrictive Practices – Monopolies and Unfair Business Practices
		eg: Professional Disciplinary Tribunals for Doctors, Solicitors Barristers etc

Courts in Scotland

CIVIL MATTERS

```
┌─────────────────────────────────┐
│ HOUSE OF LORDS                  │
│                                 │
│ Appeal Stage                    │
│ Minimum of 5 Judges             │
│ At Least 2 Scottish Judges      │
└─────────────────────────────────┘
```

APPEAL

```
┌─────────────────────────────────┐
│     COURT OF SESSION            │
│     Appeal Stage                │
│     (Inner House) (First Division) │
│     Minimum of 3 Judges         │
└─────────────────────────────────┘
```

APPEAL

```
┌─────────────────────────────────┐
│     COURT OF SESSION            │
│     Outer House                 │
│     (Second Division)           │
│     One Judge                   │
└─────────────────────────────────┘
```

RIGHT OF APPEAL FROM DECISION
OF SHERIFF PRINCIPAL

```
┌─────────────────────────────────┐
│        SHERIFF COURT            │
├─────────────────────────────────┤
│ Sheriff Principal               │
│                                 │
│ Hears Appeals from Sheriff      │
│ Court                           │
├─────────────────────────────────┤
│ ALL TYPES OF CIVIL BUSINESS     │
│ (Sheriff only)                  │
├─────────────────────────────────┤
│ SUMMARY CAUSE ACTIONS           │
│ Debts up to £1,000 and          │
│ Miscellaneous Matters           │
└─────────────────────────────────┘
```

CRIMINAL MATTERS

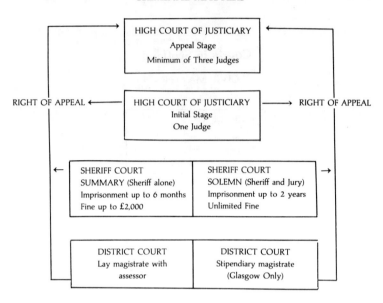

1.3 The Legal Profession

The legal profession is made up of two bodies of experts: solicitors and barristers.

Solicitors

Solicitors form the most well known branch of the legal profession. People who seek legal advice may go to a solicitor direct, or may be referred to one through some intermediate organization such as a Citizens Advice Bureau or advice service. Solicitors deal with a variety of legal matters, such as matrimonial disputes, the drafting of wills, conveyancing or employment matters. Although they cannot represent their clients' interests in the higher courts (this is normally done by a barrister – see below), they do have limited rights of audience in the magistrates' and the county courts.

In Scotland, a solicitor can appear in the district and sheriff courts for his client. A solicitor also has the right of audience in a number of other areas, for example in tribunals, licensing courts and legal aid hearings.

Many people are deterred from seeking advice from a solicitor because of fears about costs. These fears may be unfounded, particularly since you may qualify for legal aid, in which case the cost may be minimal. Some solicitors also operate what is known as a 'fixed fee interview scheme', whereby you may get a half-hour interview for a fixed fee of £5. After the allotted time the solicitor will start charging at his normal rate, about which you should ask him beforehand. Once you engage the services of a solicitor, bear in mind that you are employing and paying him or her, and you are entitled to a good service. You are also entitled to be kept informed of the various stages of your case.

The Law Society has recently launched a scheme under which a person who has been injured in an accident can have free initial advice to assess the prospects for a claim. The scheme is called ALAS – the Accident Legal Advice Service.

Barristers
(In Scotland, known as 'advocates')

Barristers never deal directly with the public, so if your case is one which must be heard in the High Court, or if it involves legal complexities, your solicitor will 'brief' a barrister who will represent you in court. Obtaining the services of a barrister adds to the expense of the case but this is standard practice. You will normally have a chance to confer with your barrister prior to the court hearing.

Barristers also assist solicitors by advising on complex points of law.

The nature of the legal profession is such that barristers are very much dependent upon solicitors for work, and for this reason they work in 'chambers' employing a clerk to deal with their financial affairs. Barristers cannot sue for their fees, and many find themselves doing work for clients and either not getting paid for it at all, or not getting paid for some time.

1.4 Legal Aid

The legal aid schemes are designed to assist you to obtain help from a solicitor with your legal problems if you have limited means. Your entitlement to legal aid will depend on your income and you will be means-tested.

Types of legal aid

There are four different kinds of legal aid:

(a) legal advice and assistance (the 'green form scheme') covers advice and assistance with any legal problem;

(b) assistance by way of representation, which covers the cost of a solicitor preparing your case and representing you in criminal and civil cases in the magistrates' courts;

(c) legal aid for civil court proceedings;

(d) legal aid for criminal court proceedings.

In addition to the above schemes, many solicitors are prepared to give up to half an hour's legal advice for £5. You are eligible for this 'fixed fee interview' whether or not you qualify for legal aid. You should ask a solicitor to confirm he offers this service before instructing him. In Scotland, this system is not in operation, although many solicitors will be prepared to discuss possible solutions to problems for a small fee.

Legal aid for civil proceedings, and legal advice and assistance are administered by The Law Societies of England and Wales, Scotland and Northern Ireland. Each country is divided into areas, each with its own Legal Aid office, and an Area and General Committee. These committees are made up of barristers and solicitors. It is the general committee which decides whether or not your application for legal aid is a reasonable one. There is a right of appeal against a refusal to the area committee. The administration of legal aid for proceedings in criminal courts is the responsibility of the Lord Chancellor's Office.

The DHSS assesses your means on an application for civil legal aid. Your solicitor assesses your means for green form advice or for assistance by way of representation. The magistrates' or Crown Courts assess your means on application for criminal legal aid.

Legal advice and assistance

This provides general initial advice from a solicitor including writing letters, making phone calls, negotiating and preparing a written case for a tribunal. The limit is £50 (or £90 for an undefended divorce or judicial separation, if you are the petitioner). In Scotland, the limit is £50, regardless of the type of case. The solicitor can apply to the Legal Aid Office for an extension to these financial limits.

If you need to go to court in civil proceedings, your solicitor may advise you to apply for civil legal aid; if the civil proceedings are in the magistrates' court, and you must apply for assistance by way of representation. If you need legal representation in a criminal case you may be advised to apply for criminal legal aid. You may obtain legal advice and assistance by signing the appropriate green form – your solicitor will advise you whether you will have to pay any contribution, based upon your savings and income.

(a) Eligibility

You must declare your savings and your income which together must come below a certain financial limit. If you are married, your spouse's savings and income will be included, unless you live apart or there is a conflict of interest between you. The financial limit is altered each year. In 1986, for the first time, the dependents' allowances were adjusted in an effort to reduce the escalating cost of the Legal Aid Scheme.

(b) Savings

When calculating your savings you can ignore the value of your home, furniture, clothes and the tools of your trade. Subtract from your savings the allowances for your dependents to arrive at your *disposable capital*, and if your savings are below the prescribed limit then you will be eligible for legal advice and assistance.

(c) Income

If you are in receipt of certain State benefits, you will be eligible for legal advice and assistance unless your disposable capital is above the prescribed limit. If your income is low then the solicitor will take your gross income and deduct income tax and National Insurance contributions. A deduction will also be made for your dependents in order to arrive at your *disposable income*.

(d) Contribution

You will not have to pay a contribution if your disposable capital and disposable income are below the current financial limits set for legal advice and assistance. Otherwise there is a sliding scale of contributions depending on your disposable income up to a set maximum, above which you no longer qualify for legal advice and assistance. You will be expected to pay this contribution at once.

(e) *Statutory charge*

Where, as a result of proceedings taken with the help of 'green form' legal advice and assistance, or legal aid (see below), money or property is received by you, or saved from being claimed by another, your solicitor must use this to pay his bill, if his bill is more than your contribution. This is called the 'statutory charge'. Your solicitor's bill is paid by the Legal Aid Office, unless the statutory charge applies. The only exception to this is that in matrimonial proceedings, the first £2,500 is exempt from the statutory charge.

Assistance by way of representation

This operates along exactly the same lines as the legal advice and assistance scheme (see above).

In Scotland, legal advice and assistance by way of representation may be given by a solicitor in respect of district or sheriff court proceedings in certain specific circumstances; however, this provision is little used in practice by Scottish solicitors.

Civil legal aid

The financial limits for legal advice and assistance, even with extensions, are very low. If your solicitor has been unable to resolve your problem quickly, he may advise you to take your case to court. Legal aid covers all the work leading up to and including court proceedings and representation by a solicitor and a barrister, if necessary. To qualify for civil legal aid, you must come within the financial limits, the grounds for taking the case to court must be reasonable and there must be reasonable prospects of success.

You can apply for legal aid even if you do not qualify for legal advice and assistance, because although the income limit for legal aid is similar to that for legal advice and assistance, the savings limit is higher. It may take several weeks for The Law Society to process your application, although emergency legal aid can be granted immediately in some circumstances, for example in cases of domestic violence.

You must declare your savings and income to the DHSS assessment officer, and they must fall below a certain limit before you can qualify. Similar provisions apply to legal aid applications as to applications for legal advice and assistance, with regard to your disposable income, disposable capital and the statutory charge.

If you do not agree with the assessment, you can ask the DHSS for a review.

All the deductions will be made from your gross income and you may or may not have to pay a contribution, depending on your financial circumstances. Any contribution may be paid in instalments if you wish.

If you win

The legal costs you pay if you win the case will depend on whether the other side is ordered to pay your costs, and if it in fact does so. It also depends on whether you are awarded any money by the court, or if you recover or preserve any property as a result of the proceedings. If the other side pays your costs in full you will probably receive at least some if not all of your contribution back.

If the other side does not pay all your costs, the Legal Aid Office will deduct the remainder of the unpaid costs from the monies which the court has awarded to you.

If you lose

If you lose you will have to pay your maximum contribution towards the costs and you may also be ordered to pay all or part of your opponent's costs. The amount you are ordered to pay will depend on your means and your conduct throughout the dispute. You will only have to pay costs where it is thought you have acted 'vexatiously or frivolously'. In such cases you will generally not have been awarded legal aid in the first place.

Legal aid is available for appeals including those from an industrial tribunal, although industrial tribunal proceedings themselves do not qualify for legal aid.

Criminal legal aid

If you have been charged with a criminal offence and you have limited means, you can receive initial advice and assistance under the green form scheme. If you need to be represented in court you can apply for criminal legal aid, which will cover the costs of the preparatory work, and the representation by a solicitor or a barrister. Criminal legal aid is also available for appeals and bail applications. Legal aid is not available for private prosecutions or the majority of motoring offences.

Juveniles are also eligible for criminal legal aid, although it is the parents or guardians who must make the application, and their income and assets are also relevant.

Legal aid is granted in criminal cases if the court decides that it is in the interests of justice to do so. This will be the case if the outcome of the charge is so serious that if found guilty, you are likely to be sent to prison or lose your job. Legal aid will also be granted if there are difficult questions of law involved; or if you do not speak English very well; or are mentally ill or mentally retarded.

If legal aid is refused you can make another application either to the court or to the Legal Aid Committee, depending on the seriousness of the case.

You may have to pay a contribution if the court decides you can afford it. Calculations based on your disposable income and capital are used to assess the amount of your contribution. You must pay the contribution to the court direct.

There are no contributions towards the cost of criminal legal aid in Scotland, and all legal aid there is now administered by a newly constituted Legal Aid Board.

1.5 Legal Expenses Insurance

The limitations on the legal aid system — its means-testing, delay, lack of comprehensive cover and provision for contributions - has led to a growth in legal expenses insurance as a means of funding litigation. Its attraction is not merely to the so-called 'middle income bracket' who do not qualify financially for legal aid, but for all those who may experience legal problems, perhaps arising from motor accidents and motoring offences, or employment disputes before industrial tribunals where legal aid is not generally available at all, irrespective of income.

The individual has in the recent past been given more and more rights, as a consumer or employee for instance, and has been made more and more aware of these rights by the media. With the decline in legal aid however, he or she has been less and less able to enforce those rights because of the rising cost of legal services — especially as he is often up against a large company, such as an employer, an insurance company or even a tour operator who was responsible for his spoiled holiday.

It is as a remedy to this dilemma that legal protection insurance finds its place by effectively balancing the scales of justice getween both parties to a legal action so far as legal costs are concerned.

A legal protection policy will pay the legal fees (up to a stated limit) incurred by policy holders, both individual and commercial, who wish to pursue or defend legal actions in a wide variety of circumstances. In addition, many companies which offer this type of insurance also include a 24 hour telephone advice line to provide vital first aid legal assistance on personal legal problems. Such services are welcomed by the consumer because they often have the effect of nipping problems in the bud before they have a chance to escalate. Their 'after hours' facility also fills a gap left by most of the other sources of advice such as solicitors, law centres and Citizens' Advice Bureaux.

Some typical headings under which cover is available are:

Personal

- Defence of all prosecutions from murder to shoplifting or careless driving
- Inheritance disputes
- Building disputes
- Home rights – troubles with neighbours etc
- Consumer problems
- Employment disputes (legal aid is not available for industrial tribunal cases)
- Claims for personal injury or death including motoring and medical negligence

Commercial

- Employment disputes
- Contract disputes
- Debt recovery
- Defence of the prosecution – for example under the Data Protection Act
- Intellectual property – copyright/licence agreements etc
- VAT and tax problems

Legal fees of up to £50,000 per incident can be covered and the basic cost of cover can be as little as £5 per year. The widest personal cover is available from around £70 per annum and commercial protection from around £100 per annum.

1.6 The Police

Police hierarchy

There are 43 police forces in England and Wales, each with a number of divisions:

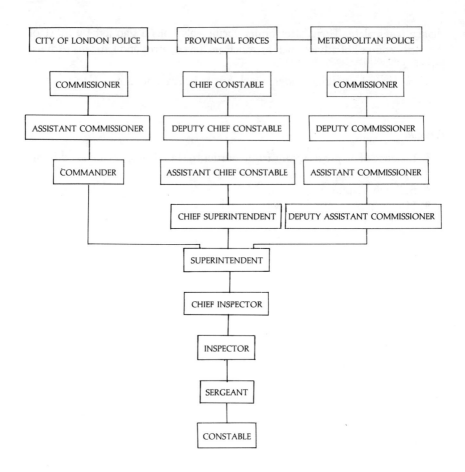

Police powers

Police powers are now largely governed by the Police and Criminal Evidence Act 1984, which has introduced a number of new powers, and filled some loopholes in previous legislation. In Scotland, the rough equivalent is the Criminal Justice (Scotland) Act 1980. Northern Ireland has special provisions to deal with the particular situation there.

Powers to stop and search

Most powers to stop and search used to be exerciseable anywhere. However, the new power created by the 1984 Act is only exerciseable in a public place. A police officer has the power to stop and search for stolen or prohibited articles. He is entitled to stop and search any person or vehicle, and anything which is on or in a vehicle provided that he has 'reasonable grounds for suspecting that stolen or prohibited articles will be found'.

The powers to stop and search must be exercised lawfully; failure to do so may make an arrest invalid. Powers exercised excessively could lead to liability on the part of the police for false arrest or false imprisonment.

In order to ensure that a suspect is treated reasonably the police should follow the 'guidelines' below, but failure to do so is not an offence:

(a) the suspect must be shown the PC's warrant card if he is not in uniform;
(b) the search must be conducted so as not to cause undue delay, embarrassment or inconvenience;
(c) the suspect must be given a record of the search in writing, within one year, if he requests one.

Other guidelines apply to the stopping and searching of vehicles:

(a) the office stopping the vehicle must be in uniform;
(b) if an unattended vehicle is searched the owner must be notified (not applicable in Scotland);
(c) a 'road check' must be authorised by an officer of the rank of superintendent or above. The person in charge of any vehicle stopped is entitled to a written statement of the purpose of the road check (not applicable in Scotland).

The police have no power of *entry* for the purpose of stop and search, and where a suspect is on private premises the owner or occupier can refuse to grant permission to enter the property. If, however, an officer wishes to enter to arrest a person then he is entitled to do so under other powers (see below).

Power of arrest

Generally, a suspect must be cautioned if he is being questioned for the purpose of obtaining evidence which may be used against him in a subsequent prosecution. A suspect must also be cautioned upon arrest for an offence and again when being charged with an offence. The caution given by the police is usually in the following terms:

'You do not have to say anything unless you wish to do so, but anything you say may be taken down and given in evidence.'

If the purpose of the questioning is not to obtain evidence, the caution is not necessary.

The Police and Criminal Evidence Act brings together into a single statute the old common law and statutory rules relating to arrest. It does, however, include some significant amendments.

In general there are three categories of power of arrest:

(a) arrest for breach of the peace – by police officers or private citizens, where a breach of the peace has occurred or is likely to occur;

(b) arrest under warrant by police officers only – this power has not been affected by the 1984 Act;

(c) arrest under statute without warrant – this may be for an arrestable offence, or where general arrest conditions apply, for finger printing or under a list of offences specifically mentioned in the Act.

The Act defines an arrestable offence, and sets out the circumstances in which a person may be arrested. The importance of the definition is that it includes a category of 'serious arrestable offence' under which the police can operate extended powers of detention, and delay access to a solicitor. The definition includes the offences which most people regard as serious, such as murder and rape, but the police also have the discretion to bring other offences, which would not normally be regarded as serious, within this definition.

In Scotland, the terminology differs, but the principles are broadly similar. If you are arrested by the police you have a number of rights:

(a) you must be informed of the fact that you are being arrested and the grounds for the arrest;

(b) you must be cautioned upon arrest (see above);

(c) you have a right to notify someone of your arrest and to see a solicitor on arrival at the police station.

Power of detention

On arrival at the police station, the suspect has to be taken to the custody officer, whose duty it is to open a custody record on the suspect and to release him if the grounds for detention no longer apply. No suspect may be released without the authority of the custody officer, and if there is enough evidence the custody officer may also formally charge him.

If you are 'helping police with their enquiries' at a police station, then until you are formally arrested, you are entitled to leave the police station when you wish.

The police have the right to detain someone for questioning without charging them, although the suspect does have the right to refuse to answer any questions.

The 'detention clock' calculates the length of time a suspect may be detained by the police without being charged. The clock starts to run from the time the suspect arrives at the police station immediately after his arrest. If he is already at the police station, the detention clock will begin to run at the time he is arrested.

Detention without charge can last for a maximum of 24 hours in the case of an arrestable offence. Anyone released at the end of the 24 hour period cannot be re-arrested unless new evidence is obtained by the police. At the end of a 24 hour period of detention without charge the suspect must be released.

The detention may be extended for a further 12 hours by a police officer of the rank of superintendent or above, but only if a serious arrestable offence is involved and the detention is necessary to secure or preserve further evidence. After the period of 36 hours the suspect must be either charged or released.

A request for a further detention of up to 36 hours can be made to a magistrate on a warrant. If the magistrate is satisfied that sufficient grounds have been made out the extension will be granted. It is then possible, using the same procedure, for the police to apply for a further extension period of up to 36 hours. The total time a suspect can be detained without charge is 96 hours. The detention must be reviewed by the custody officer after the first six hours and at regular nine hourly intervals.

In Scotland, the police are entitled to detain persons for a period of six hours without arrest where they have reasonable grounds for suspecting that that person has committed or is committing an offence punishable by imprisonment. During this six hour period, the detainee is under no obligation to answer any question other than to give his name and address.

Charging

A police officer is under a duty to charge a suspect when he is of the opinion that sufficient evidence has been obtained to prosecute. The decision as to whether the charge should be made lies with the custody officer; the suspect must receive another caution when charged.

Once a person has been charged with an offence, no further questions may be put to him with regard to the offence unless:

(a) such questioning is necessary to prevent further harm or loss to someone else;

(b) there has been some sort of ambiguity in a previous statement;

(c) such questioning is in the interests of justice.

A person detained after charge must, with certain exceptions, be released by the custody officer (usually on bail). The exceptions are where the accused's address is uncertain and the detention is necessary for the accused's own protection or where it is believed that the accused will not surrender to bail or will interfere with witnesses.

Habeas corpus

There is a fundamental right not to be held for unreasonable lengths of time in detention without being charged. Such unreasonable detention gives a person the right to apply for a writ of habeas corpus in order to secure the release of a detainee. A person who is detained after charge should be taken as soon as practicable before a magistrates' court.

A writ of habeas corpus is a written application to the High Court, making a complaint against the police for detaining a person against his will and without lawful authority. A hearing is held before a judge who may order the police to appear and justify the detention, otherwise the suspect will be released. Such applications rarely succeed.

Entry and search of premises

When entering and searching premises, the police should ensure that a number of guidelines are followed:

(a) the search must be at a reasonable hour unless this would be detrimental to the purpose of the search;

(b) the search must be no more thorough or extensive than is necessary to achieve the desired objective;

(c) the occupier of the premises should be shown due respect for his person and property during the search;

(d) the occupier will normally be entitled to have a witness present during the search, and refusal of any such request by the police would be unreasonable unless they could show that this would adversely affect the investigation;

(e) the search must be on reasonable grounds, and any force used to gain entry must not be excessive.

Search with or without warrant

In certain circumstances, usually when the police are searching for people rather than property, they have the right to enter premises to search without a warrant or the prior permission of the occupier or owner. In all cases, the search must be carried out reasonably and in the reasonably held belief that the person being sought is actually on the premises.

The provisions relating to the searching of the premises by warrant purely for the gathering of evidence, in cases where the consent of the owners is not given, are extremely complicated.

A search warrant may be granted by a magistrate following an application by the police, provided that he is satisfied that a serious arrestable offence has been committed; or that a search of the premises will produce valuable relevant evidence; and that the subject matter of the search is not 'legally privileged'.

The magistrate must also be satisfied that it is not possible to communicate with the person who can grant permission to enter the premises and that entry would be refused but for the existence of a warrant.

Searching after arrest

Having arrested a suspect, the police have the right to search their premises for articles which they believe may help with their enquiries. The search must be no more extensive than is necessary to uncover evidence relating to the offence in question. Such a search must be authorised in writing by an officer of the rank of inspector or above.

The police also have the authority to search the premises on which a suspect is arrested, even if not owned or occupied by him. The premises owned or occupied by the suspect may also be searched provided that the police reasonably suspect that they may uncover evidence relating to the crime in question and provided that the relevant officer had given his written authorisation to do so.

Seizure

Once a police officer has lawfully entered premises, he is permitted to seize anything which he reasonably believes to be evidence of a crime. The owner of the items seized is entitled to a list of the articles, and in normal circumstances, also to copies or photographs of them.

Search of persons

A person may be searched away from a police station if he represents a danger to himself or others or if, for example, he is suspected of having stolen something. The police can only ask a person to remove his outer garments. They have the power to seize and retain items found. The police must have reason to suspect the person if searching in public. This power is in addition to 'stop and search' above.

Statutory authority has now been given to the police to search people at a police station. The search must be carried out by the custody officer and a record kept. The police are not entitled to keep clothes or personal effects after the search. Intimate searches are only permissible to look for items which are hidden and could be used to cause injury, which includes drugs and offensive weapons. The search should preferably be carried out by a doctor or nurse of the same sex as the suspect.

In Northern Ireland, entry and search, and arrest and detention are governed by the Emergency Provisions Act which is reviewed annually by Parliament.

The right to legal advice and assistance

A person detained at a police station has the right to have one person told that he has been detained and where he is. If the suspect is subsequently moved, then again he has the right to inform one person of his whereabouts. However, where a serious arrestable offence is involved the police may prevent this right from being exercised for a period of up to 36 hours. The suspect must be told of this right and a record made of the fact.

The custody officer at the police station to which the suspect has been taken is bound to inform the arrested person of his right to legal advice. The detainee has the right to legal advice at any time and will be asked during his initial interview with the custody officer whether or not he wishes to exercise this right. He will have the choice of a specific solicitor, or a duty solicitor. Again the right of access to a lawyer may be suspended or delayed where a serious arrestable offence is involved but such action must be authorised by an officer of the appropriate rank, and the suspect informed of the reasons.

The suspect has the right to have a solicitor present at all interviews. Generally if he has asked for legal advice, the interview cannot commence or continue until he has received it, or until the solicitor has arrived. The solicitor may assist the suspect during the interview, for example by advising whether or not to answer questions.

The 24-hour Duty Solicitor Scheme provides for advice and assistance to be given to those arrested and held in custody, and to those who are attending voluntarily at the police station. A rota will place a specific solicitor on duty at a particular time and he/she will be under an obligation to be available. The Duty Scheme is the responsibility of regional committees of The Law Society.

Complaints against the police

Any complaints against the police should be submitted to the relevant chief officer, either by the complainant directly, or through a representative, such as a solicitor, or through the local Citizens' Advice Bureau. If the complaint is made through a representative, the complainant will have to give written consent for the complaint to be made on his behalf.

The officer to whom the complaint is made will have to make a record of the complaint, and make a decision on whether it warrants a full investigation, or whether an informal resolution would suffice.

Where it is decided that a formal investigation is necessary, an officer of a rank of no less than chief inspector must be specifically appointed to carry it out. A decision must also be taken on whether the complaint should be referred to the Police Complaints Authority. This *must* be done if it is alleged that the conduct complained of caused death or serious injury, although the chief officer has the option to refer any complaints, if he feels it necessary.

There is a slight difference in the procedure to be followed if the complaint is against a senior police officer. The investigating officer must be of at least the rank of the officer being investigated. The investigating officer's report must be submitted to the police authority concerned and the latter must then decide what further steps to take. If they are of the opinion that a criminal offence has occurred, they must submit the report to the Director of Public Prosecutions, who will decide upon charges; otherwise it is a matter of discretion for the police authority concerned.

1.7 Sentencing

The main objectives of the criminal justice system, are to prevent, detect and punish crime. To this end a 'ladder' of sentencing has been devised by the courts, not only to punish criminals, but to act as a deterrent to potential offenders. The power of the court to impose a prison sentence is usually subject to a maximum term allocated by Act of Parliament to that particular offence. The maximum term is intended to indicate the appropriate penalty for the worst case of that type; eg life for manslaughter, rape or robbery; ten years for theft; most prison terms imposed fall far below the maximum.

The sentence imposed on a criminal will depend on his age, the severity of the offence and the personal circumstances of the offender. A custodial sentence will only be imposed when absolutely necessary, and will be as short as is consistent with the need for punishment. In Scotland age is of lesser importance with regard both to responsibility and sentencing for criminal offences. There is no particular minimum age at which a child will be regarded as responsible for criminal actions.

The types of sentence which may be imposed are indicated in the table below (quoted here from *The Sentence of the Court*, HMSO 1986). Broadly identical sentences are available to courts in Scotland, except that in certain instances the name for the sentence and/or court imposing it may be different:

Age	Non-Custodial	Custodial
10–14	Absolute/Conditional Discharge Bind Over Fine ⎫ Normally Compensation Order ⎬ paid ⎭ by parent Supervision Order Attendance Centre (boys) Care Order	Not available, but see Note 1 below
14–17	Absolute/Conditional Discharge Bind Over Fine ⎫ Normally Compensation Order ⎬ paid ⎭ by parent Supervision Order Attendance Centre Care Order Community Service (over 16 years)	Detention Centre (boys only) Youth Custody (16 years) See also Note 1 below
17–21	Absolute/Conditional Discharge Bind Over Fine Compensation Order Probation Attendance Centre Community Service	Detention Centre Youth Custody See also Note 2 below
21 and over	Absolute/Conditional Discharge Bind Over Fine Compensation Order Probation Community Service	Prison

Note 1: Crown Courts alone can, in the 10 and under 17 group, award detention in a place approved by the Secretary of State for very serious offences including murder when committed under the age of 18.

Note 2: Crown Courts alone can sentence 17 to 21 year olds to custody for life.

1.8 The Crown Prosecution Service

Criminal cases are brought to court by a Crown prosecutor under the new Crown Prosecution Service. This service is publicly funded, and administered by the Director of Public Prosecutions who is in charge of the conduct of all criminal proceedings. The DDP's role is to give guidance on policy and practice and to be responsible for the overall management of the service, which has taken over the prosecution role from the police.

England and Wales are divided into areas with each area having its own Chief Crown Prosecutor. The Crown Prosecutor has the power to institute and conduct proceedings and the power to discontinue proceedings during the preliminary stages without the leave of the court. The accused must be informed of the notice of discontinuance, although he will not be given the reasons.

There is no equivalent to the Crown Prosecution Service in Scotland or Northern Ireland.

1.9 Bail

The granting of bail to a suspect means that they are allowed to go free between being charged and the trial, or between court hearings, on condition that they return to court on a specified date. In this way they have the opportunity to take legal advice and remain at work. If bail is not granted, the accused must remain in custody, and of course may lose his job. Although in most cases bail should not be unnecessarily refused, each case will depend upon its own circumstances. If bail is refused, the court must give written reasons to the applicant, who will then have to await trial on remand in prison.

Failure to return to court on the date specified as a condition of bail is a criminal offence and the accused may be subject to a fine and or imprisonment.

1.10 Contact Points

National Council for Civil Liberties
21 Tabard Street
London SE1 4LA
Tel: (01) 403 3888

An independent organization working to protect and extend human rights in the United Kingdom. It is financed by voluntary subscriptions and donations.

Police Complaints Authority
10 Great George Street
London SW1P 3AE
Tel: (01) 213 5392

Consists of a Chairman and not less than eight members, none of whom are (or have been) police officers. The members are appointed for three years at a time and two are appointed deputy chairmen. The PCA must supervise the investigation of any complaint alleging that the conduct of a police officer has resulted in death or serious injury to a member of the public. It may supervise any complaint where necessary in the public interest.

The Law Society
113 Chancery Lane
London WC2A 1PL
Tel: (01) 242 1222

Governing body for solicitors who are subject to its rules and its disciplinary powers. Ultimate sanction of removing offenders from the register.

The Law Society of Scotland
26 Drumsheugh Gardens
Edinburgh EH3 7YR
Tel: (031) 226 7411

The Law Society of Northern Ireland
90 Victoria Street
Belfast BT1 3JZ
Tel: (0232) 231614

The Solicitors Complaints Bureau
Portland House
Stag Place
London SW1E 5BL
Tel: (01) 834 2288

A body set up by The Law Society to investigate complaints of professional negligence by solicitors on behalf of their clients.

The Legal Aid Board (Scotland)
44 Drumsheugh Gardens
Edinburgh EH3 7SW
Tel: (031) 226 7061

2. The Road User

The vast increase in the use of the motor car over recent decades has brought its own problems. In this chapter, we look briefly at some of these, including buying and selling a motor vehicle, safety and maintenance, and some of the road traffic offences. Road accidents are dealt with in Chapter 7 and insurance in Chapter 8.

2.1 Buying a Car from a Dealer

When purchasing goods, the law expects you to satisfy yourself as to the quality and condition of the goods before committing yourself to the purchase, the Latin maxim 'caveat emptor' – let the buyer beware – applies. However, the law also gives you some protection, especially if you buy through a dealer.

Dealers can be licensed or unlicensed. A licensed dealer has a special arrangement (or franchise) with a particular manufacturer to sell their cars. All dealers have to satisfy a number of legal obligations under the Sale of Goods Act when selling to private individuals. These obligations form part of the contract of sale and can be relied upon should anything go wrong. In particular:

(a) the dealer must not make misleading misrepresentations (false statements or claims) about the vehicle in order to induce a sale;
(b) the vehicle should be:
 - reasonably fit for the purpose for which it has been bought – it must for example, be capable of carrying passengers from A to B,
 - of merchantable quality – in the sort of condition which a reasonable person might normally expect in a car of that age and mileage,
 - in compliance with the description offered by the dealer;
(c) the dealer must have the right to sell the vehicle.

Remember: Such key or fundamental terms form part of the contract between the buyer and the seller, and cannot be unreasonably avoided or varied.

The dealer may be a member of a Motor Agents Association (see below), and if so he should follow a number of additional guidelines contained in a voluntary code of practice when selling vehicles. For example:

- the dealer should allow the vehicle to be inspected prior to its sale;
- the dealer must accept that the checklist upon which the inspection is based may be relied upon as evidence should any dispute subsequently arise.

BEWARE: A court will not expect a second hand car bought from a dealer to be of the same standard as a new one.

How to complain

Remember: It is usually the seller of the vehicle who is liable for any fault, and not the manufacturer (see *Product Liability*, page 119).

If you buy a car from a dealer and you have problems with it, your legal rights will, if all else fails, be protected by the courts. However, before considering taking the matter to court you should exhaust the following practical alternatives:

(a) *The dealer*
As soon as you become aware of the problem, you must notify the dealer, in writing, telling him of your complaint. If the fault is serious and occurs very soon after purchase, you may be entitled to return the car and demand a full refund.

(b) *The Motor Agents Association*

If the dealer concerned has failed to settle the matter satisfactorily, you should pproach the Motor Agents Association for some assistance — provided that the dealer is a member. The MAA operates an arbitration scheme by which a dispute may be settled and in any event, is a helpful 'go between'.

(c) *Warranties and guarantees*

Cars very often have warranties attached to them on sale. A warranty is an undertaking by the dealer to accept responsibility for faults on certain major parts. The warranty acts in a similar way to a guarantee in that it extends your legal rights, but cannot restrict or replace them. You should read the terms and conditions of the warranty carefully to ensure that you are aware of what will be covered should anything go wrong.

Your legal remedies

If you can prove that a dealer has broken any of the legal obligations as to quality and fitness, you may be able to:

(a) *Reject the vehicle and reclaim the purchase price*

You must not delay in notifying the dealer, preferably in writing, of your intention to reject the vehicle. This right is available only if major defects are discovered shortly after delivery, so any delay may lose you the right, leaving only the possibility of claiming damages. Do not do anything which may be regarded as inconsistent with the intention to reject, such as having the vehicle repaired or accepting offers of compensation from the dealer. If you have announced your intention to reject the car, do not carry on using it as this may damage your case.

(b) *Claim for damages*

If, for whatever reason, you lose your right to reject the vehicle, you may sue for damages - such as the cost of repairs that are necessary to put the car in a satisfactory condition, the cost of alternative transport for the duration of loss of use of the car and various other expenses which may have been incurred.

2.2 Buying from a Private Individual

The term 'caveat emptor' applies more strictly to a purchase from a private individual, since you are in a much weaker legal position than if you buy from a dealer. This is usually reflected in the price at which the vehicle is being offered for sale, since cars are usually cheaper if bought privately.

BEWARE: The only legal obligation on the private seller is not to make misrepresentations or false statements, for example as to the mileage or general condition of the car, in order to induce a sale.

If misrepresentation occurs then your ultimate right will be to reject the car and sue for damages.

If you are unsure about the condition of a vehicle, have an independent inspection carried out by a professional body such as the AA.

Remember: Whoever you buy from, it is illegal to sell a car which is unroadworthy. It is equally unlawful to take an unfit vehicle onto the public highway. The result of doing so is a possible fixed penalty of £24, or, if taken to court, a fine of up to £1000 (more usually £50), and the addition of three penalty points to the driving licence. This does not apply if the car is not for use on the highway.

2.3 Finance

HP agreements

If you buy a car under a hire purchase agreement, it is actually the finance company which buys the car from the dealer, and retains legal ownership of it. It then hires it to you for the repayment period, and during this time stands in your shoes with regard to getting legal rights enforced. The finance company remains the legal owner of the car until completion of the HP agreement, when ownership passes to you. You can pay off the loan earlier if you wish to do so.

Default and repossession

If you default on the repayments to the finance company, you will find that they wish to repossess the car. However, as a debtor, you will be protected against a repossession action by the Consumer Credit Act 1974, which offers the following safeguards:

(a) the finance company must give you notice in writing of their intention to repossess the vehicle in order to give you the opportunity of catching up with the payments;

(b) the finance company must obtain a court order before they can enter your premises to repossess;

(c) 'protected goods' may not be repossessed without a court order. Goods are 'protected' if;

- the buyer under the HP or conditional sale agreement has defaulted; and
- at least one third of the total amount due under the agreement has been paid; and
- the seller has retained 'property' in the goods, see below.

In normal circumstances, a seller who does not own the goods cannot pass on a good title when he sells. However if you buy a car in good faith, not knowing that there is an HP agreement on it already, you *will* acquire ownership of the car and it cannot be repossessed by the finance company.

Conditional sale agreement

Under a conditional sale agreement you are *committed* to buying the vehicle on completion of the agreement. As under HP, there are legal provisions with regard to the finance company having the right to repossess the car on default. Again, the car does not become yours until completion of the agreement.

Credit sale agreement

When purchasing through a credit sale agreement, the trader sells the car to the finance company, who sells it to you. You immediately acquire ownership of the car, along with the right to sell – unlike goods bought on HP. You will be required to pay off the outstanding instalments before resale. The finance company cannot repossess the car if you default on the payments, but will pursue the loan through the courts in the normal way.

Do's and don'ts on buying cars

Do:
- consult a competent expert *before* agreeing to buy;
- make sure you are able to afford the required repayments if you are buying on a finance agreement;
- check the history of the car with the seller before buying, eg mileage, past owners, accidents, or outstanding claims on the car;
- make sure that the MOT, excise licence and insurance requirements are complied with before you test drive – you can be prosecuted as a user for any non-compliance.

Don't:
- hand over the purchase price until arrangements have been made for delivery or collection of the car;
- rely on the seller's word that the car is not under any form of finance agreement, or that if there is one he intends to discharge it before he sells it to you. If the seller defaults on the payments, you may lose your money, and the car. The Citizens' Advice Bureau (CAB) will be able to check whether or not the car in question is subject to an HP agreement.

2.4 Selling a Car

If you are selling a car as a private individual, the implied conditions as to quality and fitness do not apply to you. However, you should be careful in your description of the car since you may be sued if you mislead the purchaser.

Make sure you are paid in cash or by a banker's draft — if you are paid by cheque, you may face problems with clearance.

2.5 Auction Sales

BEWARE: Auctioneers are not liable for any defects in the vehicle, no matter what condition they are in. If the auctioneer is selling on behalf of a business, the obligations as to merchantable quality and fitness for purpose still apply. If the goods are being sold on behalf of a private individual, the legal requirements do not apply and the buyer will have no protection, unless he can prove misrepresentation by the seller and this will only be possible if you can identify the seller and prove misrepresentation. In practice this may be very difficult.

In all auction sales, the sale is not binding on the purchaser until the auctioneer's hammer falls. If the seller at an auction has put a reserve price (a minimum price) upon the goods he wishes to sell, then the auctioneer cannot sell them until that price has been reached — if he allows the hammer to fall before this price has been reached, the sale will be invalid.

2.6 Repairs and Servicing

When you instruct a garage to carry out repairs or other work, you enter into a contract with that garage. If you have expressly asked the garage to carry out specific work and they agree to your instructions they must fulfil their obligation to you.

In addition to carrying out your express instructions the garage must comply with a number of implied conditions under their contract with you. These are as follows:

(a) all parts and materials fitted or supplied by the repairer must be owned by the repairer;
(b) all parts must meet any description by the repairer; if he says he will fit a particular type of tyre, he must fit that type alone;
(c) the parts must be of merchantable quality and reasonably fit for the purpose for which they have been supplied;
(d) the repairs must be carried out with reasonable care and skill and within a reasonable time.

Wherever possible a garage should give you a written quotation for the cost of any major repairs. The quotation should also state whether or not VAT has been included. If you accept a written quotation from a garage, both you and the garage are bound by it.

Estimates, unlike quotations, are not binding between the garage and yourself. In order to ensure there are no nasty shocks, ask the garage to let you know if the work to be carried out is to cost more than the estimate, *before* they carry out the work.

If you are faced with a high bill or are dissatisfied with the work, complain to the garage owner or manager straight away. If your complaint cannot be remedied immediately, you may have to pay the bill to get your car back, since the garage has a 'lien' on the car and may lawfully keep it until payment has been made. You may then sue for the overcharging.

Checklist: repair and servicing

- make sure the garage you choose is competent;
- get a written quotation which includes parts, labour and VAT;
- ensure that the work they carry out will be guaranteed, either for a specified length of time or for a certain number of miles;
- if you are having a service carried out, find out exactly what is included in the cost;
- give a clear and, if necessary, written description of what you want the garage to do;
- agree on the length of time the car is to be kept in;
- leave your telephone number and ask the garage to contact you if they feel that they have to exceed the quotation. If they do not get your permission, you will not have to pay the additional costs.

How to complain

(a) Make a formal complaint, in writing, to the garage owner. Be sure to keep a copy of all correspondence.

(b) If you are not satisfied, take your complaint to the Trading Standards Department of your local Council, or if you are a member, to one of the motoring organisations.

(c) If the garage is a member of a trade association, contact them for assistance. They may be able to sort out the dispute for you by way of arbitration.

(d) If the garage is not a member of a trade association (or you do not wish to use their arbitration scheme), you will have to take your case to court. You should seek advice from the local CAB or your solicitor.

2.7 Documentation

All vehicle owners must obtain the following documents before the car is permitted to go on the road; otherwise they will be committing criminal offences.

Insurance: Under the Road Traffic Act 1972, you are required to have as a minimum third party insurance, although most motorists choose between third party fire and theft and fully comprehensive. Insurance is dealt with in more detail in Chapter 8; see page 151.

Tax Disc: This may be obtained from a post office on production of an insurance certificate and if appropriate, a current MOT certificate. The disc should be displayed in the bottom near-side corner of the windscreen.

The penalty for failing to have a valid tax disc is usually a fine equal to three times the amount of the duty lost. If you have a disc, but fail to display it, you could be fined a fixed penalty of £12.

MOT Certificate: All cars which are more than three years old must be examined for major faults every year. A detailed check list must be gone through by a qualified mechanic and anything which does not come up to the required standard must be rectified before the car will be given an MOT. There is a statutory charge laid down by the Ministry of Transport for this testing.

Failure to obtain a test certificate will result in a likely fine of £20 (maximum £400), although no penalty points will be issued.

BEWARE: An MOT certificate is merely an indication of the condition of the car at the time of the test. It should *never be relied upon as evidence of the condition of a car you wish to purchase.*

Driving Licence: The type of licence needed and your entitlement to it depends on:

- the type of vehicle to be driven;
- whether you have passed a driving test;
- your age and health;
- your past driving record.

The minimum age requirements for taking a motor vehicle onto the public highway vary according to the type of vehicle in question:

16 – moped (up to 50cc) or invalid carriage
17 – motor cycle
       car

agricultural motor vehicle
18 – public service vehicle
medium sized heavy goods vehicles (from 3.5 tonnes to 7.5 tonnes)
21 – heavy goods vehicle

At the age of 70, your driving licence can be renewed every three years provided that you disclose any disabilities and, if necessary, consent to a medical examination.

If you require a heavy goods licence, additional tests must be passed, and a separate licence obtained. A licence which allows you to drive a car will not entitle you to drive heavy goods or public service vehicles.

If your circumstances alter to such a degree that the facts stated on the application for the driving licence change – for example if you suddenly become ill and no longer fit to drive a vehicle – you must notify the DVLC in Swansea immediately.

A provisional driving licence allows a learner driver to gain road experience prior to taking the driving test. A full driving licence may be applied for when the test has been passed. Any person driving while holding a provisional licence must display 'L' plates on the vehicle, both front and back. Learners are not allowed on motorways, nor are they permitted to drive a vehicle unless there is a qualified driver with them.

2.8 Taking your Car Abroad

There are obvious problems when taking your car abroad, like language difficulties and driving on the right-hand side of the road. Many pitfalls can be avoided by taking basic precautions.

Driving licence

It must be a full licence and you may need to obtain an international driving permit which is obligatory in some countries.

Insurance

Your British insurance policy will not necessarily cover you while abroad. Check the small print. If necessary obtain an International Motor Insurance Card (known as a 'green card') from your insurance company to extend your cover to the countries you are visiting. Make sure that you are covered for unforeseen garage bills and personal injury.

Different laws

Try to familiarise yourself with the local laws; motoring organisations can help.

Speed limits

May be different (and in any event will be in kilometres, not miles per hour). Minimum speed limits exist in some continental countries, especially on motorways, and are rigorously enforced; some exist in the UK too.

Lights
May have to be adjusted for driving on the right.

Documents

Take all your driving documents (licence, insurance, MOT, registration document). Be careful not to leave them in the car in case they are stolen. You will have a better chance of recovering your car if the relevant documents are still in your possession.

Traffic offences
You may be fined on the spot in some countries. It is usually cheaper to pay on demand, unless you are insured to enable you to get legal advice.

In case of an accident

Take with you a red triangle sign in case of an accident. Familiarise yourself with the procedure to be followed if an accident should occur. In some countries your car will be impounded and a large deposit will be required to get it back. You can insure against this.

If a claim is made against you for injury or damage, pass it on to your insurer when you return home. If you wish to claim against someone, the claim can only be made in the foreign court and in accordance with their laws. This will take time and will be expensive. Make sure your insurance covers you for this.

2.9 Car Hire

If you hire a vehicle, you will normally be liable for any loss or damage caused by negligence. You should make sure that you read the agreement you sign to ensure you know what your position is.

Hire firms can be prosecuted for failing to ensure that their vehicles are in a roadworthy condition.

But *beware*, this will not prevent you from being prosecuted for driving a vehicle which is unroadworthy, even if it is not owned by you.

2.10 Car Parking

Car parks

Generally, you park at your own risk and, apart from your own insurance, you will have no remedy for any damage to your vehicle while in the car park, unless you can prove negligence on the part of the car park operators. In many cases, operators try to limit their liability for damage to your car by means of an exclusion clause in their contract with you. Quite often this is printed on the ticket issued to the customer. To be effective, such exclusion clauses must be fair and reasonable in the eyes of the law, and must be drawn to the attention of the customer.

Remember: an exclusion clause cannot exclude liability for personal injury or death; any attempts to do so being inoperative.

Street parking

There are a number of restrictions on street parking all of which are contained in the Highway Code. For example, where there is a single yellow line on the kerbside, it means that parking is not allowed within specified times, except for loading and unloading goods. Double yellow lines mean that there is a total ban on parking at any time of the day or night. It is also an offence to park anywhere which may cause an obstruction to other vehicles or pedestrians.

2.11 Road Traffic Offences

A number of regulations govern the way in which motor vehicles are driven on the highway. Serious contraventions often lead to police prosecution of the offending motorists. Such prosecutions are more often successful than not, with most motorists pleading guilty and receiving the appropriate number of penalty points (see below). Alternatively, or in addition, a fine may be imposed, and more rarely, imprisonment ordered.

The delay and expense involved in this system led to the introduction of the new fixed penalty system on 1 October 1986, extending the system which originally applied only to parking offences to a wide variety of other offences. The less serious, non-endorsable, offences are now subject to a fixed penalty of £12, and an endorsable offence is subject to a £24 fine. As an incentive to pay quickly, the fine will be increased by 50 per cent if it is not paid within 28 days of issue of the ticket. This system does not apply in Northern Ireland.

Alternatively the motorist may use his right to contest the matter in court, but risks much higher penalties should he lose the case. If the licence has to be endorsed, it must be sent to DVLC at Swansea to receive the relevant number of penalty points.

The police have the discretion whether to issue the fixed penalty or to prosecute – the more serious the offence, the greater the chance of prosecution.

The principal motoring offences are noted below with the penalties which may be incurred. The points which are endorsed with each offence are in brackets. An accumulation of 12 points within a three year period will result in disqualification.

Seat belts

It is an offence for anyone travelling in the front seat of a car not to wear a seat belt. It is the person who fails to wear the seat belt who commits the offence, so the driver cannot be prosecuted for the passenger's failure to adhere to the law.

It is an offence to allow a child under 14 to travel in the front passenger seat without wearing a seat belt; the driver or owner of the vehicle will in such circumstances be liable. Over 14 it is the child who is liable. Babies under 12 months old may not travel in the front seat. Children too young to be protected by seat belts must be carried in special child restraints.

- Maximum penalty: £100 fine
- *Likely fine*: £15
- Fixed penalty: £12

General maintenance

Brakes: must be kept in good working order and there must be a handbrake which works

Lights: must be kept clean and you should check regularly that all the bulbs are in working order

Tyres: must be carefully maintained (minimum 1 mm tread) and free of cuts in the fabric; pressure must be checked regularly

Wipers/washers: must be kept in working order and windows must be kept clean

Steering: must be in good working order

Exhaust system: must be in good working order. It must not be too noisy

Horn: must be in good working order
Mirror: must have at least one mirror to see traffic behind

There is a variety of penalties for these offences. For example, having defective brakes or defective steering attracts a maximum £1000 fine, 3 penalty points, a likely fine of £50; or a £24 fixed penalty.

Causing death by reckless driving

- Maximum penalty: 5 years imprisonment
- Obligatory disqualification and endorsement (4 points)

Reckless driving

- Maximum penalty: 2 years imprisonment
- Possible disqualification
- Obligatory endorsement (10 points)
- *Likely fine:* £300

'Reckless' means driving so dangerously that a serious and obvious risk of damage or personal injury is created. The term 'reckless' should be distinguished from 'careless', and the distinction is often very fine. Careless driving is doing so without due care and attention and as such is not as serious as reckless driving, but is still serious enough to receive heavy penalties. Every case is dependent upon its facts, but if it can be shown that the driver acted carelessly, at least some degree of blame will be apportioned to him. Usually the court will rely upon the evidence of independent witnesses to the incident, particularly where the case is not so clear cut.

Careless and inconsiderate driving

- Maximum penalty: £1000 fine
- Possible disqualification
- Obligatory endorsement (2-5 points)
- *Likely fine:* £60 (extremely variable)

Failing to stop after an accident and give particulars or report an accident

- Maximum penalty: £200 fine
- Possible disqualification
- Obligatory endorsement (4-9 points)
- *Likely fine:* £125

Driving without a licence

- Maximum penalty: £400 fine
- Possible disqualification and endorsement depending on circumstances (2 points)
- *Likely fine*: £75

Driving with uncorrected defective eyesight or refusing to submit to a sight test

- Maximum penalty: £400 fine
- Possible disqualification
- Obligatory endorsement (2 points)
- *Likely fine*: £25

Using vehicle without minimum legal insurance cover

- Maximum penalty: £1000 fine
- Possible disqualification
- Obligatory endorsement (4–8 points)
- *Likely fine*: £125

Speeding offence

- Maximum penalty: £400 fine
- Possible disqualification – if speed limit is exceeded by more than 30 miles per hour; disqualification probable for speeds over 100 mph
- Fixed penalty: £24
- Obligatory endorsement (3 points)
- *Likely fine*: £2.50 for every mile per hour over the limit

2.12 Drink and driving – to be safe, don't drink and drive

The maximum permitted levels of alcohol while driving are as follows:

- 35 microgrammes of alcohol in 100 millilitres of breath;
- 80 milligrammes of alcohol in 100 millilitres of blood;
- 107 milligrammes of alcohol in 100 millilitres of urine.

The police have the right to stop a motorist if they suspect he or she is under the influence of alcohol.

A conviction for a drink/driving offence usually brings with it an automatic disqualification. The disqualification period is generally 12 months, but may be longer, depending on the severity of the offence. If a further conviction follows within 10 years, a further ban of three years will be imposed. In the most severe cases, drivers may have to provide medical evidence that there is no drink problem before the licence can be returned.

Disqualification may be avoided in very limited circumstances, for example if the motorist can prove that the alcohol had been put into his drinks without his knowledge, or that he was responding to an emergency and could not avoid drinking and driving. However, these defences are extremely difficult to establish.

The importance of a professionally presented plea in mitigation should not be underestimated – your job could depend on it.

Breath tests

The roadside breath test is used primarily as a means of separating those motorists who are under the limit from those who are over it. It is only those who exceed the limit on the test who are arrested and taken in for further tests. Anyone who refuses to submit to a breath test will be arrested and taken to the police station.

In Scotland, there may be some police stations which do not yet have facilities for electronic breath testing. At these stations, the police may require a blood or urine sample. The procedures outlined below will then apply.

Only uniformed officers can give the roadside breath tests. If you are asked to take part in the test, you must co-operate. If you have smoked a cigarette during the 10 minutes preceding the test, or if you have consumed an alcoholic drink during the 20 minutes preceding the test, you should tell the officer, since this may affect the meter reading.

Once you have been arrested and taken to the police station, you will be required to take a further two breath tests – the lower of the two readings will be required upon by the police in any prosecution proceedings.

If the second breath test gives a borderline result, or if the breath-testing machine is not working at the time the test needs to be taken, an alternative sample of either blood or urine has to be taken. A sample of blood may only be taken with your consent, and the test must be carried out by a doctor. If a conviction arises from the test, you may have to pay the doctor's fee.

Two samples are taken, and one has to be given back to the motorist for private analysis, if he so wishes. If the police fail to offer a sample to the motorist, they will be unable to use the one they keep.

Remember: A motorist who fails to provide the necessary samples when requested to do so, will be guilty of an offence and liable to a penalty of up to £2000 and possible disqualification for up to 18 months.

Driving or attempting to drive when unfit through drink or drugs

- Maximum penalty: 6 months imprisonment, £2000 fine, or both
- Possible disqualification and endorsement (4 points)
- *Likely fine*: £200

The motorist will be regarded as driving even though stationary at the time he is challenged by the police. If the vehicle cannot move as a result of damage, or if it would be impossible for the motorist to drive because of injury, the charge of attempting to drive while unfit to do so will still be applicable.

Whether the motorist is unfit is a question of fact which must be supported by medical evidence.

Being in charge of a motor vehicle when unfit through drink or drugs

The term 'being in charge' is open to interpretation and has caused much legal argument. The motorist is still considered 'in charge' of the vehicle even if found inside it sleeping off the effects of the alcohol. It is the same if the motorist is found to be walking to the vehicle in possession of the keys. However, if the motorist can prove to the court that there was no possibility of driving the vehicle while over the permitted limit for alcohol or drugs, this may be a defence.

- Maximum penalty: 3 months imprisonment, £1000 fine, or both
- Possible disqualification
- Obligatory endorsement (10 points)
- *Likely fine*: £100

Driving or attempting to drive with excess alcohol in breath, blood or urine

- Maximum penalty: 6 months imprisonment, £2000 fine, or both
- Obligatory disqualification and endorsement (4 points)
- *Likely fine*: £200

Being in charge of a motor vehicle with excess alcohol in breath, blood or urine

- Maximum penalty: 3 months imprisonment, £1000 fine, or both

- Possible disqualification
- Obligatory endorsement (10 points)
- *Likely fine*: £100

Failing to provide a specimen of breath for a breath test

This refers to the roadside breath test, refusal of which is an offence.

- Maximum penalty: £400 fine
- Possible disqualification
- Obligatory endorsement (4 points)
- *Likely fine*: £50

Failing to provide a specimen for analysis or laboratory test

This is a separate offence and refers to a refusal at a police station. Penalties will differ according to the offence with which the motorist has been charged – driving or attempting to drive with excess alcohol and then refusing to provide a specimen; or being in charge and refusing to provide.

- Maximum penalty: 6 months imprisonment, £2000 fine, or both
- Possible disqualification
- Obligatory endorsement (4–10 points)
- *Likely fine*: £200

2.13 Contact Points

Complaints about cars

The Conciliation Service
Motor Agents Association
201 Great Portland Street
London W1N 6AB
Tel: (01) 580 9122

Deals with complaints about second hand cars and motor bikes, and offers an arbitration service for members and customers

The Customer Relations Advisor
Society of Motor Manufacturers and Traders
Forbes House
Halkin Street
London SW1X 7DS
Tel: (01) 235 7000

Deals with complaints about new cars and will arbitrate between consumer and trader/manufacturer

Customer Complaints Service
Scottish Motor Trade Association
3 Palmerston Place
Edinburgh EH12 5AF
Tel: (031) 225 3643

Deals with complaints about second hand cars and motor bikes

The Conciliation Service
Vehicle Builders and Repairers Association
Belmont House
Finkle Lane
Gildersome
Leeds LS27 7TW
Tel: (0532) 538333

Deals with complaints about repairs to cars and caravans by garages

Motoring organisations

AA
PO Box 50
Fanum House
Basingstoke
Hampshire
RG21 2EA
Tel: (0256) 20123

AA
Fanum House
Erskine Harbour
Erskine
Renfrewshire PA8 6AT
Tel: (041) 812 0144

RAC
RAC House
Lansdowne Road
Croydon CR9 2JA
Tel: (01) 686 2525

RAC (N. Ireland)
RAC House
79 Chichester Street
Belfast BT1 4JR
Tel: (0232) 240261

RSAC
11 Blythswood Square
Glasgow G2 4AG
Tel: (041) 221 3850

Driver and Vehicle Licensing Centre

DVLC – England, Wales & Scotland
Swansea SA6 7JL
Tel: (0792) 72134

DVLC – N. Ireland
The Department of the Environment
Vehicle Licensing Central Office
County Hall
Coleraine
BT52 3HS
Tel: (0265) 4133

Department of Transport

2 Marsham Street
London SW1 3EB
Tel: (01) 212 3434

Scotland:
Scottish Office
Department of Transport
New St Andrews House
Edinburgh
EH1 3SX
Tel: (031) 556 8400

Northern Ireland:
Northern Ireland Office
Department of Transport
Stormont Castle
Belfast BT4 3ST
Tel: (0232) 63011

3. The Home

This chapter looks at some of the more important aspects of the law relating to the home. After a discussion of buying, selling and renting, we look briefly at home improvements, trespass and nuisance, and the responsibilities of the occupier to visitors and others.

3.1 Buying and Selling a Home

When buying or selling property through estate agents or privately, contracts are never binding at law until the principal terms of the contract are put in writing, signed, dated and exchanged. After exchange, but before completion, it is possible to withdraw from the contract, although you would lose any deposit you had paid and you may be sued for breach of contract.

Before entering into any contract for the purchase of property you should ensure that:

(a) you have the property surveyed to be certain that it is structurally sound and you are paying a reasonable price for it;
(b) the conveyancing is carried out by a competent solicitor or licensed conveyancer;
(c) you have received a formal offer from a bank or building society regarding your mortgage and that you will be able to cover all incidental costs, such as stamp duty and legal fees.

Preliminary matters

If you are buying your property with the help of a building society or bank loan, a survey will almost certainly have to be carried out before the finance will be handed over, to satisfy the lender that the investment is sound. You can ask for the property to be valued, or for a fuller survey to be carried out if you wish. It is generally advisable to opt for the full survey where older or unusual properties are involved. It is also possible to have an independent survey carried out, the advantage being that an independent surveyor is working specifically for you and if at a later date (having relied on the survey report) structural problems arise, it will be possible to sue the surveyor for any loss incurred.

If you are buying and selling property you should not exchange contracts on the house you are buying until you have exchanged contracts on the house you are selling. 'Chains' of properties being bought and sold often build up and the risk of the chain breaking should one of the transactions fall through, could lead to the necessity for an expensive, 'bridging loan'.

BEWARE: If you make misleading or false statements when selling your property privately, the buyer may take you to court for misrepresentation.

If you are selling through estate agents the agents try to protect themselves from such action by incorporating a blanket disclaimer into the written description of properties they are selling. Even so, the estate agents must avoid blatant misrepresentation (ie the inaccurate statement of material facts rather than opinions) in order to avoid liability under the Misrepresentation Act. Whether the blanket disclaimer will be upheld in court will depend upon whether it is fair and reasonable.

Deposits

There is no obligation to pay a deposit when an offer to purchase a property has been made. If the seller or his agent asks for a deposit, the purchaser may refuse. If, however, a deposit is paid, a receipt should be obtained and the money only handed over on the understanding that it is returnable if the contract falls through. A deposit should preferably be paid to a 'stakeholder' for both parties, not simply to the seller's agent.

Upon exchange of contracts, the purchaser will be asked to pay a deposit on the property. This is usually 10 per cent of the purchase price, but it could be less depending upon what is agreed between the buyer and the seller. This deposit is forfeited if, after exchange, the purchaser fails to complete the contract.

In Scotland, it is rare for deposits to be required, although you may find they are required in connection with builders' 'missives'. If a deposit is required,

The contract

The contract which is drawn up for the sale and purchase of property is the most important part of the transaction – it is the written agreement which forms the basis of the sale.

In Scotland the contract is known as a 'missive'. The formal letter or missive is exchanged between the parties' solicitors.

The contract identifies the property being sold, who is buying and who is selling, the price, deposit paid and any 'extras' which have been included in the sale. It also gives the date upon which completion is to take place, and the interest which will be charged if completion is delayed. The contract includes other conditions of sale which are more general and apply to every conveyancing transaction.

Solicitors representing both parties will exchange drafts of the contract before agreeing on the final version, which is then ready to be signed, dated and exchanged. Also prior to exchange, the solicitor will have satisfied himself that enquiries made of the local authority and the seller's solicitor do not reveal anything adverse.

In Scotland, contracts or 'missives' are formed by negotiation and exchange of formal letters between the parties' solicitors until both reach agreement on the terms of purchase or sale. Initially, an offer to purchase is submitted. The seller's solicitor discusses this offer with his client, and then sends a qualified Letter of Acceptance. The purchaser's solicitor then consults his client, and if the qualifications are acceptable, a formal letter concluding the bargain will be sent. When that letter is sent, the missives form a contract with no right to back out. If either party does back out, he will be liable to meet the expenses incurred by the other side, including legal expenses for the re-sale of the property, and possibly the difference in the price obtained if this is substantially lower than the original contract.

Exchange and completion

After exchange of contracts the solicitor must make investigations as to the owner's title to the property. If the property is unregistered, he must check through old conveyances to find a line of title going back at least 15 years. If the property is registered at HM Land Registry (and eventually all property will be so registered), he must check the 'office copy entries' from the Land Registry to ensure that the seller is in fact the owner. If all is well, the mortgage documents are signed and everything is then ready for the day of completion. On completion old mortgages are paid off, the balance of the purchase price is paid and the deeds and the keys are handed over to the purchaser.

In Scotland, there is no limit on the time over which title will be checked. A competent solicitor will carry out a thorough investigation of the title by checking conveyances back to the original construction of the property.

Conveyancing costs

It is now possible, since the solicitors' 'monopoly' on conveyancing has been broken, to go to either a solicitor or a licensed conveyancer for your conveyancing. There are advantages in going to a solicitor, not only in terms of experience and skills, but also because solicitors are obliged by their professional body to insure themselves against any negligence claims which may be brought against them. The Law Society has also set up a Solicitors Complaints Bureau, which will be able to assist anyone who has a complaint against their solicitor.

It is also possible to sue licensed conveyancers if negligence can be proved but compensation may be limited. Licences for conveyancing are issued by the Council of Licensed Conveyancers only to those applicants who have practised conveyancing for at least 10 years. Very high standards are imposed by the Council, to which members must adhere.

Conveyancers may also be members of the National Association of Conveyancers which acts as a trade association with powers to discipline members following complaints.

It is advisable to contact a number of solicitors with a view to ascertaining potential fees. Some may issue written quotations, which distinguish between their actual fees and other necessary expenses, such as stamp duty, land registration fees and other disbursements. However, a conveyancing agent might be cheaper and it definitely pays to shop around.

An estate agent's commission will vary according to the type of agreement between the seller and the agency. Lower rates are offered if they are the 'sole agents' for the property, but the terms should be checked.

3.2 Guarantees

National House Building Council

New houses usually have the advantage of a National House Building Council (NHBC) warranty, which offers protection against faulty workmanship, usually for a period of up to 10 years. However, the existence of the warranty does not mean that the purchaser should dispense with a survey, since the warranty does not apply to all defects for the full 10 years. Protection is offered during the first two years for all serious defects except normal wear and tear and normal shrinkage, although certain electrical defects are only covered for one year. After the initial two-year period has elapsed the remaining eight years of the scheme cover only major structural defects. The extent to which the builder is liable is limited to the amount the first owner of the house paid for it, up to a maximum of £50,000, together with a small allowance for inflation.

All defects for which the builder is held liable must be rectified within 14 days.

Damp and timber treatment

Such guarantees usually last for a period of up to 25 years, and the existence or otherwise of a guarantee should be ascertained by a prospective purchaser before the sale takes place. To be of value the guarantee should apply to, or be capable of being transferred to, all future owners of the property and not only to the person who had the treatment carried out.

3.3 Joint Ownership

Where property is bought by more than one person, for example by a husband and wife, they normally own the property as 'joint tenants'. The alternative is to purchase as 'tenants in common' and it is important to choose the right method for your particular situation. Ideally both possibilities should be discussed at an early stage with a solicitor. Incidentally, the use of the word 'tenant' in this context is for historic reasons, and is not to be confused with someone paying rent under a letting agreement (see below).

A joint tenancy implies 50/50 division of the purchase price or sale proceeds and, on the death of one of the parties, gives automatic 100 per cent ownership to the survivor.

A tenancy in common divides the purchase price or sale proceeds between the parties in accordance with their contributions. Each then owns that specific share, which forms part of his property or 'estate' on death, and can therefore be left to someone other than the remaining tenant in common.

In Scotland, the concept of 'tenants in common' is unknown in owner-occupied property. Each spouse will have proprietorial rights if the title is in joint names. If the title is in the name of only one spouse, matrimonial occupancy rights exist.

3.4 Renting Property

Rent Acts

The majority of tenants are covered by the Rent Acts, which are designed to protect tenants from eviction or excessive rents, and to ensure that the landlord fulfils his legal obligations towards the tenant. The provisions of the Acts are highly complex, but the simplest method of ascertaining if you are protected is to check that the following conditions apply:

(a) the tenancy must be of a residential dwelling rather than a hotel or guest house;

(b) the tenant must have exclusive possession of at least one room in the property (this provision does not necessarily apply in Scotland);

(c) the rateable value of the tenant's part of the property must have been less than £750 in April 1973 (£1500 if in Greater London);

(d) the rent must be at least two thirds of the March 1965 rateable value of the tenant's part of the property.

The property must not be:

(a) a holiday let;

(b) let with substantial board;

(c) provided because of your employment.

To complicate matters further, even if the Rent Acts do apply, they may offer either full or restricted protection to the tenant.

The Rent Acts will not apply if the landlord lives on the premises and provides services such as cleaning and cooking. This is known as a 'restricted contract'.

If you have problems with your landlord and your position is unclear, seek legal advice.

Remember: You cannot be evicted without a court order.

If you think your rent is too high either you or the landlord can apply to the Rent Office for a fair rent to be registered. This rent will then be the maximum the landlord can charge for the next two years. See 'Fair Rents', on page 52. In Scotland, the tenancy must be a 'protected tenancy' within the meaning of the Rent Acts before an application can be made to a rent officer.

Tenancy agreements

A tenancy may exist without a formal written agreement, although it is common for a landlord or an agent to draw up a formal document (known as a lease or tenancy agreement). You should always read such documents to ensure that you accept all the provisions and conditions before signing it. Anything with which you do not agree may be negotiated, and amended with the agreement of the landlord. This document will contain the conditions and obligations of your tenancy (some of which are covered below) and will be referred to should any dispute arise between you and the landlord.

In Scotland also the tenancy is binding without a written agreement, although it might prove difficult to establish that a tenancy agreement exists if nothing has been put in writing. There are specific provisions in the law for such agreement, but if you are in doubt, you would be well advised to consult a solicitor.

Landlord's responsibilities

If you pay weekly, the landlord has a duty to provide a rent book stating the name and address of the landlord and the amount of rent payable. If you pay at longer intervals you are not legally entitled to a rent book, although where there is no rent book a receipt should always be obtained for the rent, as this may be the only proof of legal tenancy.

Arguments over the responsibility for repairs and maintenance are one of the most common causes of dispute between landlord and tenant. If you lease property for seven years or more, responsibility for repairs, such as damage caused by natural ageing, weathering or normal wear and tear, should be set out in the rent agreement. However, for 'short lets' of under seven years, the landlord is responsible for all structural and external repairs, and also for repairs and maintenance to all sanitary and heating appliances. It is possible to take court proceedings to force the landlord to undertake repairs.

When the property is rented as furnished accommodation, the landlord is bound to ensure that it is to fit to live in when the tenancy commences. Accidental damage is usually your responsibility, and it is advisable to insure against this.

Remember: The landlord can be responsible only for repairs that he has been told about. Always make requests in writing, and keep a copy of your letter.

Tenant's responsibilities

If you are responsible for internal decorations and repairs, the extent of this responsibility should be stated in the tenancy agreement. If the agreement states that you should keep the property in 'good repair' you have a duty to maintain it in at least the condition in which you found it. Make a note of the decorative condition when you move in, in case you are faced with a bill for 'dilapidations' on departure, with no way of checking their accuracy.

Failure to adhere to the terms and conditions of a valid tenancy agreement could result in your eviction, if the landlord can prove to a court that the agreement was properly entered into and that you have breached the terms of your lease. In certain circumstances, the landlord may retain the property of the tenants to meet his liabilities.

Shorthold tenancies

A shorthold tenancy is one fixed for a term of between one and five years. During the period of tenancy the tenant has full protection under the Rent

Acts. At the end of the term of tenancy the landlord has a right to repossess the property if he wishes.

To create a shorthold tenancy certain conditions must be fulfilled:

(a) the letting must be for a fixed term of between one and five years;
(b) the letting must be a new let;
(c) the landlord must serve a 'shorthold notice' on the tenant before the tenancy is granted (a specimen of a shorthold notice can be obtained from the CAB);

A shorthold tenancy cannot be converted into a fully protected tenancy after the term has expired. The tenant has no right to remain at the end of the fixed term, provided the landlord gives the tenant proper notice, and the court will give the landlord possession against the tenant.

Fair rents

A fair rent is one which has been assessed by a rent officer and has been recorded in the rent register which is available for inspection at the local council offices.

Either the landlord or a tenant can ask for the rent to be assessed. When setting the rent the rent officer will consider the area, the state of repair of the house, its age and the quality and quantity of furniture provided. If the landlord or tenant is dissatisfied with the rent registered they may appeal to the Rent Assessment Committee to re-examine the matter.

A registered rent remains in force until a new registration application is made. This cannot be made within two years after the previous registration unless:

- there is a joint application by landlord and tenant; or
- there has been a substantial change of circumstances.

Letting your home temporarily

The Rent Act makes provision for you to have your home back if you let it on the understanding that you will wish to return to it at some future date. You may give yourself the right to return at the end of the agreed term, and if the tenant refuses to leave, you will be able to apply to the court for a possession order, which *must* be granted provided that you have complied with the necessary conditions.

In order to take advantage of this, you must give the tenant written notice before the tenancy commences or on the day it commences, that you intend to repossess under the relevant provisions of the Rent Act.

When wishing to regain possession you must either serve the appropriate notice on the tenant, or wait for the fixed term to expire. If you have any problems you may apply to the court, which in urgent cases will deal with your case within two weeks.

Letting your retirement home

You will also be protected under the Rent Act if you wish to let the home to which you intend to retire. The conditions are broadly similar to those outlined above, but when you wish to gain possession you must, generally, have retired from your regular full time employment.

Sub-letting

There are often restrictions on sharing rented accommodation with others. The majority of short term tenancy agreements prohibit sub-letting, although some agreements allow it with the landlord's permission. If permission is unreasonably withheld, you may take the matter to court to overrule the landlord's decision.

Sharing rented accommodation

Where a number of people share rented accommodation, in order to ensure that each tenant has the protection of the Rent Acts, each person's name must appear on the rent book. All parties to the tenancy should be aware of the conditions of the tenancy and be aware that they are responsible for their share of the bills.

If only one person's name is on the rent book, the others paying 'rent' to that sole tenant, then only the person named on the rent book will have the protection of the Rent Acts. If that person decides to leave, the others will have no protection and may be evicted by the landlord.

If you use an accommodation agency to find property to rent you will not be obliged to pay them anything unless and until you have accepted a property on their books. Normally such agencies charge a week's rent for their service and it is illegal for them to try and charge you before you have accepted one of their properties.

Notice

You should give written notice to your landlord when you wish to leave the property. The length of notice will be determined by the tenancy agreement and the type of tenancy.

As a tenant you are entitled to a notice to quit in writing, which must give you at least four weeks' notice and information about your legal rights. The tenancy agreement cannot change the above rules. If there are no special provisions in the tenancy agreement the notice must bring the tenancy to an end at the end of a complete period of tenancy (for example, at the end of a month, if a monthly tenancy). You do not have to leave when the notice to quit runs out. You cannot be lawfully evicted until the landlord obtains a possession order from the courts. Illegal eviction is a criminal offence.

Whether or not the courts will grant the landlord a possession order will depend on the type of tenancy you have. You should seek legal advice as soon as you receive a notice to quit.

Insurance

The landlord is responsible for the insurance of rented property. You must insure your own personal belongings, and should also insure interior decorations. The tenant is not responsible for insuring the actual premises, unless it is otherwise stated in the lease that you should do so, but you should check that the landlord has some insurance cover and ideally ascertain the extent of it.

3.5 Home improvements

Before improving your home, a number of important factors must be considered:

Finance

There are three methods by which you may be able to raise the money required for improving your home:

(a) *Local authority grant*

If your home needs modernising you can apply for a grant, whether you are owner, landlord or tenant. There are 4 different grants available:

- improvement grants given at the discretion of your local authority, for major improvements such as providing kitchen or bathroom facilities;
- intermediate grants for smaller improvements such as the installation of toilet, hot and cold water and associated repairs and replacements;
- repair grants for substantial structural repairs on older properties;
- special grants (not available for tenants), for putting in other standard amenities and means of escape, if necessary.

Such grants are not as freely available as they once were and will only be awarded if very stringent requirements are met by the applicant.

(b) *Mortgage extension*

You should contact your building society or bank and apply for an extension to your current mortgage. A survey will usually have to be carried out before the money will be granted.

(c) *Bank or building society loan*

Special rates are available for home improvement loans, on which tax relief may be claimed.

Legal aspects

Get your solicitor to check the deeds to see if there are any restrictive covenants on the property which may be breached by your proposed improvements. For example, there may be a covenant forbidding any alterations to the existing buildings. If the property is leasehold it may be necessary to obtain the permission of the leaseholder to carry out the proposed alterations.

In cases where the property was purchased with the assistance of a mortgage, it may be necessary to consult the lender before undertaking any improvements or alterations – the insurance company will also have to be informed since the improvements may affect the premium.

Planning permission and building regulations

Planning permission is generally required from the local authority to undertake major structural changes to your property. Such permission is not required for the following forms of improvement:

- internal improvements or alterations which do not affect the exterior of the building;
- changes on the land surrounding the property, for example, the construction of a swimming pool in the garden;
- extension of the property, provided that the extension does not increase the overall size of the building by more than 10 per cent;
- the construction of a garage or other out-building provided that the 10 per cent limit is adhered to;
- the erection of boundary walls or fences which are not more than two metres high at the side of the property and one metre at the front.

Even if planning permission has been obtained, it is still necessary to conform to the building regulations, which state the manner in which the work is to be undertaken, particularly in terms of safety. Usually each stage of the work must be approved by the building inspector from the local authority before the next stage may be started.

Beware: Never rely on the local authority inspector's approval of the work done as an indication that it is satisfactory. If you are not happy with the work carried out by the builder, always get your own survey. If you are eligible for a local authority grant for the improvements, do not pay any money to the builder until you have notice of the grant in writing.

Remember: Building disputes are one of the most common sources of litigation, so make sure you choose a reputable builder, preferably one who is a member of the Federation of Master Builders (see page 61) or other trade association.

Any firm you engage to do the improvement to your home, or indeed to provide any service will be bound by the Supply of Goods and Services Act - see Chapter 5, page 107.

3.6 Offences relating to property

Committing a wrongful act under the civil law towards another person or their property, is called a tort (in Scotland a *delict*). Below are examples.

Trespass

Whether you own or rent the property you occupy, you have a legal right to enjoy it without interference. If anyone disturbs that enjoyment by entering onto your property without consent (whether actual, implied or by law), they are trespassing. You may obtain an injunction (in Scotland, known as 'an interdict') to prevent this, and may also claim damages. Although reasonable force may be used to evict trespassers, it is advisable to leave the resolution of the matter to the police and the courts.

Trespass is a civil wrong, and offenders can only be sued, and not prosecuted, since they are not committing a criminal offence. However, they may be prosecuted if they trespass on property belonging to dockyards, railways and military establishments, since this amounts to the offence of criminal trespass.

New legislation has been introduced to give the police further powers to evict mass trespassers from private land. The legislation is designed to speed up the civil procedure, and also makes such a trespass a criminal offence in certain cases.

The Public Order Act 1986 gives the police the power to disperse mass trespassers in certain limited circumstances, provided a number of criteria are satisfied. In order for the power to be exercisable, two or more people must enter the property unlawfully, with the common intention of remaining there. The occupier or someone acting on his behalf, must have taken reasonable steps to remove the trespassers, who must have caused damage to property on the land or have used threatening or abusive behaviour to the lawful occupants.

Rights of way

If there is a public right of way over private land, it gives the public right of access along certain permitted routes without committing trespass. If the route allows access by car, it is known as a highway; if it can be used only by pedestrians, it is a footpath, and if it can be used for cycling or riding, it is a bridleway. Local authorities have the power to designate certain paths as public rights of way. The land may also be 'dedicated' as a footpath by the landowner, either expressly or by tradition.

Once a right of way has been established, the landowner has very limited rights to plough it. There is a statutory right to plough in the interests of 'good husbandry', as long as steps are taken to repair the footpath as soon as possible.

Whoever is in charge of a right of way is obliged to keep it free from obstruction, and must also place a signpost at the point at which the right of way joins a normal highway, stating what type of path it is.

The landowner is not permitted to keep a fierce or wild animal to prevent the public gaining access to a right of way, although a bull may be put in a field through which there is such a right of way, provided that the bull is of a non-dairy breed, or that it is accompanied by cows or heifers, or it is less than 10 months old.

It is permissible to take animals across public rights of way, provided that they are kept under control, and on a lead when crossing a field with livestock in it. A landowner is entitled to shoot a dog which worries its livestock, and the owner responsible for the animal may be prosecuted.

Generally the public also have a right to cross 'common' land, moorland (although the right may be restricted during hunting seasons), most country parks, beaches and picnic sites owned by the local authority and/or the National Trust.

It may be a criminal offence to pick wild flowers or fruit growing on land to which the public have access, although it may be permissible by custom to pick certain fruits such as blackberries, provided that normal routes are kept to.

In Scotland, legal rights of way are much more limited, although most mountain and moorland is generally freely accessible.

Children

Children are treated as a special case, so if you have a feature on your property which could attract children, for example a pond or quarry, you must take extra precautions. The fact that you put a sign up warning of dangers may be of no significance to a young child, and if some form of injury befalls the child, you may be liable.

Squatting

Squatting is a particular form of trespass. It involves setting up home in someone else's unoccupied house without their consent. It is not a crime unless some form of violence is used or threatened in order to gain access to the property. If a squatter has taken up residence, the 'displaced residential occupier' is permitted by law to use reasonable force to get him out. The owner will also be able to obtain a court order for repossession of the premises.

In Scotland, the concept of 'squatting' does not exist. The only near equivalent is 'an occupier without right or title' and there is a specific form of civil action for the removal of such a person from the premises.

Nuisance

Whether you own or rent the property you occupy, if anyone spoils your enjoyment of living there, for example by making excessive noise, and that interference is unreasonable, they are creating a nuisance.

Frequently problems arise between next door neighbours, often due to the inadequate construction of their houses. Other common complaints include interference with television reception, overhanging trees and noisy animals or children. Each of these may constitute a nuisance, but whether such complaints are actionable in the courts will depend upon the degree of interference and the inconvenience suffered. If you bring a successful court action, you may be entitled to compensation for the damage you have suffered as a result of the nuisance. This may be combined with an injunction to stop the nuisance from continuing or recurring.

A nuisance can be either private or public, the difference being that the former affects a person in his own home, and the latter interferes with people at large and can be a crime as well as a tort.

In practice it may be difficult to establish liability for a public nuisance, since it is necessary to prove 'fault' in the form of unreasonable conduct on the part of the defendant. You must prove greater damage to yourself (special damage) than that suffered by the public at large, and that the special damage was the direct result of the nuisance in question, in order to succeed in the tort of public nuisance.

3.7 Occupier's Liability

Any person who owns or rents a property owes a duty of care to anyone who lawfully enters that property to ensure that the premises are reasonably safe. It is usual for an occupier to insure against this liability. The occupier must ensure that any dangerous defects are repaired promptly and that notices are displayed if there is a danger of any harm coming to a visitor. Greater care is required if small children are at risk. However, an occupier is not liable for defects of which he had no knowledge. Nor, generally, is an occupier liable to trespassers or squatters, but see the paragraph on children, page 60.

3.8 Removals

Before engaging a firm to undertake your removals, you should shop around and obtain a number of quotes in order to get the best deal. During the move itself, the removal firm will owe you a duty of care, and must take all necessary precautions to look after your property. Should there be any damage then it will be up to you to try and prove that the firm was negligent in order to get compensation from them.

Because of the nature of the business, many firms try to impose terms on their customers which will exclude them from liability should anything be lost or damaged. It is always advisable to take out your own insurance cover in these circumstances just in case anything goes wrong.

3.9 Contact Points

Professional bodies

Architects Registration Council of the UK
73 Hallam Street
London W1N 6EE
Tel: (01) 580 5861

Registers all architects, and issues a code of conduct for members. Also investigates complaints of serious misconduct, and refers less serious matters to RIBA (see below). Has the power to strike offending architects off the register to stop them practising.

Royal Institute of British Architects
66 Portland Place
London W1N 4AD
Tel: (01) 580 5533

Professional body for architects, but membership is voluntary. Can offer general advice on architectural matters and fees charged. Has Code of Practice for members and will investigate any suspected breaches. Serious matters will be referred to the Architects Registration Council.

Incorporated Association of Architects and Surveyors
Jubilee House
Billing Brook Road
Weston Favell
Northampton NN3 4NW
Tel: (0604) 404121

Professional association which will advise members of the public on technical matters, and can recommend members. Will also investigate complaints against members, and can sanction where necessary with warnings or disciplinary hearings.

National Association of Conveyancers
44 London Road
Kingston-upon-Thames
Surrey KT2 6QF
Tel: (01) 549 3636

Deals with complaints against members who fall below the required standards set by the Association. Also has complaints procedure and disciplinary powers.

Council of Licensed Conveyancers
Golden Cross House
Duncannon Street
London WC2N 4J
Tel: (01) 210 4559

Issues the licence to conveyancers who satisfy the requirements. Deals with complaints against conveyancers and has the power to discipline or revoke licence.

Federation of Master Builders
33 John Street
London WC1N 2BB
Tel: (01) 242 7583

Complaints against members should be made in writing and will then be investigated. An arbitration scheme is available, and protection is also offered to customers who have had work carried out under the warranty scheme should their builder become insolvent within 2 years after the work has been carried out.

National House Building Council
Chiltern Avenue
Amersham
Bucks HP6 5AP
Tel: (02403) 4477

Will investigate complaints of faulty workmanship on houses covered by a certificate. A conciliation service is available if both parties agree to be bound by the decision of the conciliator; otherwise the dispute may go to arbitration. The council can discipline or strike off offending members.

Department of the Environment
Building Research Establishment
Garston
Watford WD2 7JR
Tel: (0923) 676612

Part of the Department of the Environment. Will offer free telephone and written advice on any building faults if brief, otherwise will make a charge.

Brick Development Association
Woodside House
Winkfield
Windsor
Berkshire SL4 2DX
Tel: (0344) 885651

Deals with technical problems raised by members of the public or the building trade.

The Countryside Commission
John Dower House
Crescent Place
Cheltenham GL50 3RA
Tel: (0242) 521 381

The Commission's brief is to promote conservation of the countryside and promote the public's right to the country. It will assist the public with related problems.

Estate agents

Any complaint should be directed to whichever body the estate agent belongs to. They all issue similar codes of conduct and operate a disciplinary procedure. Problems are investigated and could in serious cases lead to a warning being issued or a full disciplinary hearing.

General Practices Division
Royal Institute of Chartered Surveyors
12 Great George Street
Parliament Square
London SW1P 3AD
Tel: (01) 222 7000

Incorporated Society of Valuers and Auctioneers
3 Cadogan Gate
London SW1X 0AS
Tel: (01) 235 2282

National Association of Estate Agents
Arbon House
21 Jury Street
Warwick CV34 4EH
Tel: (0926) 496800

Building societies

Building Societies Ombudsman
Grosvenor Gardens House

35 Grosvenor Gardens
London SW1X 7AW
Tel: (01) 931 0044

Investigates complaints against societies. However, most societies have their own internal complaints procedure which must be exhausted before any approach can be made to the Ombudsman.

Repairs and improvements

Heating & Ventilating Contractors Association
ESCA House
34 Palace Court
London W2 4JG
Tel: (01) 229 2488

Trade association formed to ensure that standards of installation are as high as possible, and operates a guarantee scheme to protect members of the public against contractors who become insolvent during or after installation. Will arrange for another contractor to finish or repair the installation at no extra cost. Also offer an arbitration scheme.

British Chemical Dampcourse Association
16a Whitchurch Road
Pangbourne
Reading RG8 7BP
Tel: (07357) 3799

Trade association dealing with complaints and acting as mediator between customer and member. Also operates guarantee scheme for customers who deal with members who become insolvent.

British Wood Preserving Association
Premier House
150 Southampton Row
London WC1V 5AL
Tel: (01) 837 8217

Will provide the public with technical advice and a list of members. Has Code of Practice for members and will conciliate in the event of a dispute.

External Wall Insulation Association
National Cavity Insulation Association

National Association of Loft Insulation Contractors
Draught Proofing Advisory Association Ltd
PO Box 12
Haslemere
Surrey GU27 3AN
Tel: (0428) 54011

Represents major manufacturers and some contractors. Will supply list of members to the public and if necessary can refer disputes to arbitration.

Glass and Glazing Federation
44/48 Borough High Street
London SE1 1XB
Tel: (01) 403 7177

Trade association which provides technical advice to the public and its own members. Also has a complaints service which settles disputes through its own conciliation service or through arbitration, and operates a deposit indemnity scheme which refunds or transfers deposits paid where a member becomes insolvent.

British Decorators Association
6 Haywra Street
Harrogate HG1 5BL
Tel: (0423) 67292

Provides a free internal arbitration scheme involving members and may assist in investigations against non-members, for which a small fee may be charged.

Removals

British Association of Removers Ltd
277 Gray's Inn Road
London WC1X 8SY
Tel: (01) 837 3088

A trade association formed to impose and maintain high standards for members, which will deal with complaints against members, and in serious cases will arrange for arbitration, and if necessary has the power to revoke membership.

Noise

The Noise Abatement Society
PO Box 8
Bromley
Kent BR2 0UH

4. The Family

This chapter is devoted to some important elements of the family and family life: marriage and marriage breakdown; the special place of children in the eyes of the law; medical matters, including mental health; and, finally, death.

4.1 Engagement

During the course of an engagement, you are legally entitled to cancel the wedding, or the engagement, at any time. Any presents received during the engagement are treated in the same way as wedding presents: those received from his family are his to keep, and those received from her family she can keep.

In the absence of anything agreed to the contrary, if the woman has received a ring from the man, this is regarded as her property, and on termination of the engagement, she may keep it if she wishes. Money spent on wedding preparations cannot be recovered by either party.

In Scotland, gifts by either party to the other are not recoverable should the wedding be cancelled, although certain gifts in contemplation of marriage, for example, an engagement ring, may be recoverable if the marriage is broken off without legal justification. If the engagement is broken off by the agreement of the parties, all gifts should be returned, and in all cases gifts from relatives and friends should be returned if the marriage does not take place.

4.2 Marriage

Generally speaking, anyone over the age of 18 is legally entitled to marry if they wish. Anyone between the ages of 16 and 18 wishing to marry, must first of all obtain the consent of their parents or legal guardian.

In Scotland, anyone over the age of 16 is legally entitled to get married if they wish, without the consent of their parents or legal guardians.

Additionally the parties must:

(a) be free to marry (not already married to someone else);
(b) be of opposite sexes;
(c) marry in accordance with certain legal procedures;
(d) not be blood relatives, although they may get married if they are related only by marriage.

If these legalities are not complied with the marriage may be declared void from the outset and be annulled. Voidable marriages and divorce are dealt with later, see page 76.

All marriages must be registered with the Registrar General via his local district registrar. Although it is not necessary to obtain a marriage certificate at the time of the wedding it is advisable to do so, since there are a number of circumstances in which a marriage certificate is necessary. However, copies can be obtained at a later date if required.

Church marriages

Before a marriage can take place in a Church of England church, the proposed wedding must be announced in the parish churches of the districts in which you both live, so that anyone who knows of a reason why the wedding should not take place has the opportunity to object. This procedure is known as 'publishing the banns', which must be read out in the church on three consecutive Sundays. You must then marry within three months of the last reading of the banns – if you do not get married within this time, the banns will have to be published again.

Alternatively, you may apply for a common licence to marry, which is granted by the diocesan bishop and is valid for three months. You must have been resident in the parish in which you wish to marry for at least 15 days in order for the licence to be granted.

You may also apply for a special licence, which can only be granted by the Archbishop of Canterbury, and which allows the marriage to take place anywhere and at any time.

With regard to religious marriages in Scotland, the requirement of reading or otherwise of the banns is largely decided by each individual church. Your local minister will advise, but there are likely to be residence qualifications.

In a marriage between Roman Catholics, however, the widespread practice is a requirement that banns be read in the home parish of each party on three consecutive Sundays, as close to the date of marriage as possible, although there is no limit between the reading of the banns and the marriage.

Civil marriages

If the marriage does not take place in a Church of England church, a Superintendent Registrar's certificate *must* be issued, and this may be done with or without a licence. If the certificate is issued without a licence, the marriage can take place 21 days after you have given notice of your intention to marry to the registrar, provided you have been resident in the area for a minimum period of seven days.

If the certificate is issued with a licence, the marriage can take place on the first day after the notice has been given, provided that you have been resident in the area in which the marriage is to take place for a minimum period of 15 days.

Generally a marriage ceremony must take place in a registered building within the district in which one of the marriage partners lives, between the hours of 8 am and 6 pm.

In Scotland, you must give notice to the registrar or registrars of the district or the districts where you usually reside or have resided for 15 days prior to the proposed marriage. A public notice is displayed at the Registry Office for seven days prior to the marriage. If no objections are lodged with the registrar, he will issue a certificate of publication of notice, which is the equivalent of a proclamation of the banns. In certain circumstances, a sheriff's licence may be obtained. The marriage must take place within 10 days of that licence, and all marriages must be registered with the registrar of the parish in which they took place within three days of the date of marriage.

Marital rights and obligations

Usually the wife takes her husband's surname but there is no legal obligation on her to do so.

Upon marriage the Inland Revenue must be informed of the change of status, and the change of name in the case of a wife, as should other interested bodies such as banks, building societies and your employer.

Finance

Each spouse has a legal obligation to maintain the other and any children of the union. Upon divorce this continues in respect of the children until they finish full-time education. The husband no longer has any obligation to pay his wife's debts other than, possibly, for household necessities.

Upon marriage the husband becomes entitled to a married person's tax allowance, and the wife remains entitled to the single person's allowance. A married couple can only obtain MIRAS tax relief on mortgages up to

£30,000 between them. The named parent is entitled to receive any Child Benefit.

Property

The Matrimonial Homes Act gives a wife certain legal rights to occupy the matrimonial home even if she is not the legal owner or tenant. These rights can be registered to protect her position. On divorce, the wife will generally be entitled to a share in the matrimonial home or proceeds of its sale.

If the house is owned by two people as 'joint tenants' (see page 51), then upon the death of either spouse, the entire ownership of the property goes to the surviving spouse. During the marriage, both parties are responsible for the mortgage, even if one of them has no income.

4.3 Bigamy and Polygamy

If either one of the parties to the marriage turns out to be already married, the marriage will be bigamous and void. It is fairly unusual for such offences to result in prosecution, but if there is evidence of fraudulent or malicious behaviour, prosecution will result.

The courts of this country will recognise polygamous marriages if they were legal in the country in which they took place, even though such marriages are illegal under our own law.

4.4 Co-habitation

(In Scotland, known as 'marriage by habit and repute')

Finance

Unmarried couples living together lose the right to be treated as single persons for supplementary benefit purposes - the supplementary benefit rate for a couple is lower that that for two single people. Co-habitees are assessed separately for tax purposes. However, if there are two or more children, each parent is entitled to claim additional relief as a single parent. Each person may also claim mortgage relief up to a maximum of £30,000.

If a co-habitee father leaves the woman with his children he must maintain the children. In some cases it may be necessary to have the father declared as such by an affiliation prior to seeking a maintenance (in Scotland, 'aliment') order for the children. If the man denies that he is the father, blood tests may be taken to establish paternity.

Property

If the parties own the home jointly, then on sale they are entitled to the net proceeds of sale on a 50/50 basis, unless they bought in different proportions and hold the property as tenants in common (see page 51), in which case the proceeds of sale are divided in accordance with the contribution each has made.

If the property is owned by one of the co-habitees, then the non-owning co-habitee may face great difficulty on sale in claiming a share, even if the relationship has been long-standing. The non-owner may need to use the law to show either direct financial contribution (mortgage payments) or indirect contribution (by payment of other bills, or by time and effort devoted to improving the property). Each claim is judged on its merits.

If the co-habitees live together in rented accommodation, any rights they have will depend upon which one of them is the tenant. If only one of the parties is the tenant, that person known as a 'sole tenant', and the other party will be a licensee, and as such will have no independent right to occupy the property. The sole tenant will be the only party who has a lawful right to occupancy. The sole tenant may give the licensee reasonable notice in writing to quit the property, and if he refuses to go, the tenant may go to court to obtain an eviction order.

If the property is occupied by the co-habitees jointly, both have a right to occupy, and cannot get the other out. Both will be liable for the whole of the rent and not just their share of it.

On the death of one partner, the other may, if financially dependent on the deceased, seek provision from his/her estate whether or not there was a will. Legal advice must be obtained on this. Ideally both parties should make proper provision during their lifetime by means of a will.

4.5 Domestic Violence

In addition to remedies available to victims under the criminal law, battered wives (including co-habitees) and children can seek an injunction (in Scotland, an interdict) from the civil courts to stop the violent behaviour from recurring. The court may order the violent person to stop the violence and/or to stay away from the matrimonial home for a specified period of time. The injunction may also apply to personal possessions contained in the house.

Although in most cases the man against whom the injunction is being sought will be notified of the court proceedings, if it is an emergency, the application may be made without his knowledge ('ex parte').

A court also has the power to issue an 'ouster injunction' or an 'exclusion order' which will order the offending party to leave the matrimonial home, and prevent him entering for a specified period of time. Breach of this order can result in imprisonment.

If the injunction is not obeyed, the person to whom it applies may be imprisoned. Legal aid may be obtained for injunction proceedings and legal advice should be sought as soon as violence, whether threatened or actual, occurs.

4.6 Termination of Marriage

Divorce

Divorce proceedings are started by a petition, which 'prays' or asks for a divorce. The petitioner issues the petition to the respondent through the court. In cases of adultery the third party is known as the 'co-respondent', and if known, is named in the proceedings. It is not possible to obtain a divorce within the first year of marriage (two years in Northern Ireland). After that, the petitioner must prove that there has been an irretrievable breakdown in the marriage, based on one of the following facts:

(a) adultery by the respondent;
(b) unreasonable behaviour by the respondent to the petitioner, which the latter finds intolerable;
(c) the couple has lived apart for a total period of two years, and divorce is by agreement;
(d) desertion of the petitioner by the respondent for two years;
(e) the couple has lived apart for five years.

In Scotland, it is permissible to apply to the court for a divorce at any time provided cause can be shown.

Except in Northern Ireland, it is not essential to consult a solicitor when commencing divorce proceedings, unless there are areas of contention, such as custody of the children, maintenance or property.

If there are any children of the marriage, satisfactory arrangements must be made for them. To this end another form, the 'statement of arrangements for children', must be completed. This form is then submitted to the court together with the petition and the court fees, when the divorce proceedings commence.

In Scotland, the procedure is different. In divorces based on two years separation with consent, where there are no children under the age of 16 and where there is no financial claim, a simplified divorce form can be obtained from your local sheriff court. A similar form can be obtained and used in respect of five years separation without the other party's consent. In relation to divorce on some other ground, you would be advised to consult a solicitor.

All undefended divorces (those in which there is no dispute about there being grounds for divorce, even if other matters such as money or children are in dispute) are heard in the county court (in Scotland, sheriff court).

A defended divorce is one in which the respondent denies the fact that the marriage has broken down, or challenges the alleged grounds. Such cases are heard in the High Court (in Scotland, the Court of Session or the sheriff court). The respondent may also oppose the granting of a decree nisi on the grounds that dissolution of the marriage would result in grave financial hardship to the respondent. This only applies in cases where the divorce is brought on the grounds of five years separation without consent, and that in all the circumstances of the case it would be wrong to dissolve the marriage. In England and Wales, the Divorce Registry in Somerset House also acts as a divorce county court and divorce proceedings may be started there.

Divorce procedure

A special procedure is followed in the majority of undefended divorce cases, which ensures that the divorce is dealt with as quickly as possible. A problem free divorce takes approximately four months from beginning to end.

If the registrar is satisfied that the marriage has irretrievably broken down and that the grounds for the divorce have been proved, he signs a certificate which clears the way for the granting of a decree nisi. Such a decree is issued by a judge in open court although it is not necessary for the parties to attend.

If the registrar is not satisfied that the marriage has broken down, he directs that the case should be heard in open court with the parties in attendance.

The petitioner can apply for the decree nisi to be made 'absolute' six weeks after the decree nisi has been granted. This is not issued by a judge, but is stamped by the court and sent to the petitioner or the petitioner's solicitors.

The minimum six week period between the decree nisi and the decree absolute acts as a breathing space for both parties in case of second thoughts. This six week time limit may be extended if the arrangements for the children are not approved by the judge. Once the arrangements have been approved, the judge issues a declaration of satisfaction which enables the petitioner to apply for the decree nisi to be made absolute. The respondent may apply for the decree to be made absolute if the petitioner has not done so within three months.

In Scotland, in undefended divorce cases, the procedure is firstly to reach agreement on the ancillary matters. If agreement cannot be reached, the case will proceed as defended. If agreement is reached, the solicitors for the pursuer will lodge in court 'affidavits' or sworn statements relating to the breakdown of the marriage and the arrangements for any children. A sheriff will then consider these statements, and if satisfied that all is in order, with particular reference to the arrangements for children, will grant decree of divorce. This is not done in open court and attendance of the parties is unnecessary. The court will then forward the decree to the parties or to their solicitors.

Separation

An informal or judicial separation may be preferred to a divorce by some couples, possibly on religious grounds, since after the judicial separation, the parties remain technically married. If both parties agree to the separation, they may go to a solicitor to have a formal agreement drawn up regarding the division of matrimonial possessions, maintenance and custody of children. This agreement should be registered in the magistrate's court to obtain tax relief on the payments. Alternatively, a judicial separation can be sought in the county court (in Scotland the sheriff court), in the form of judicial separation proceedings, which releases the parties from their obligation to live together, but does not terminate the marriage.

Annulment

In some circumstances a marriage can be annulled; it can be declared void or it may be voidable. A *void* marriage is one which was illegal at the outset, and in fact never existed at law. A *voidable* one is where the actual marriage ceremony was valid, but the marriage subsequently become invalid.

Void marriages are those where the couple:

(a) are too closely related (although they may be related by marriage);
(b) are under the age of 16 at the time of the marriage;
(c) did not follow the marriage formalities correctly;
(d) are of the same sex; or
(e) one of them is already married at the time the ceremony takes place.

If any of the above apply, the innocent party will have the option to annul the marriage.

A voidable marriage is one which:

(a) has not been consummated because one of the partners is incapable of sexual intercourse;
(b) has not been consummated because of the wilful refusal of one of the parties to consummate it;
(c) took place without the consent of one of the partners;

(d) took place when the woman was pregnant by a man other than her husband and the man was ignorant of this fact until after the marriage;

(e) took place when one of the couple had a venereal disease.

The petition on such grounds must be filed within certain time limits after the marriage took place.

Maintenance payments

Each spouse has the right to maintenance from the other so long as the marriage exists. When a marriage breaks down, the couple may agree to voluntary maintenance payments. If not, an application for maintenance can be made to the court as part of the divorce proceedings. If there are no immediate plans to divorce, an application for maintenance can be made to the magistrates' court. Maintenance payments can also be sought for the children of the marriage.

If the couple are not married then the obligation to maintain only exists in relation to the children of the union.

In considering what the maintenance payments will be the court looks at the gross incomes of both parties and their outgoings and responsibilities. It also considers the house and other capital assets, the earning capacity of the parties, and the age and duration of the marriage. The court places particular emphasis on the welfare of the children and the desirability of the partners becoming financially independent.

The court also has the power to divide up the family assets such as the home, possessions and savings.

The maintenance order enables the paying party (usually the husband) to claim tax relief on the amount paid. An application to vary the order can be made at any time by either party. The order will exist for a specific period, usually until co-habitation or remarriage or until the children complete their full time education. Increasingly, however, maintenance orders for the spouse are becoming more difficult to obtain, and if granted, may be only for a short period.

Conciliation

In many cases during the breakdown of a relationship, couples may be referred by a solicitor to a branch of the National Family Conciliation Council, which may help them to reach an agreement, particularly where there are conflicts over children and financial matters. It may also be used in cases where the fact that the marriage has broken down is disputed by one of the parties.

The aim of the conciliation service is to discuss the outcome of the breakdown, and not to seek a reconciliation, although this may in fact come about.

Presumption of death

If one marriage partner has had no contact with the other for a minimum of seven years, the other may be presumed dead, and the remaining party will be permitted to remarry if they wish.

It is advisable to check with Somerset House whether a divorce has been granted to the 'disappeared' party. A small fee is charged for this service.

Custody of children

This issue will have to be settled in court if the parents cannot come to some agreement on their own. The best interests of the children are the prime consideration of the court. All evidence to be presented is put in the form of sworn statements (affidavits) and served on the parties so that they and the judge may be fully aware of the facts of the case.

The granting of legal custody will give the parent to whom it is given the right to make important long-term decisions which affect the child, particularly with regard to education, medical treatment and moral and religious upbringing.

Actual custody (care and control) refers to the duty to care for the child on a day-to-day basis.

An access order grants permission for the non-custodial parent to visit the child on a regular basis.

Joint custody is where both parents have legal custody, but one of the parents is given care and control over the child, and the other is granted 'reasonable access'. This ensures that although the child is living with only one of the parents, any major decisions are taken by both parents.

A disputed custody case is usually heard in private by a county court judge in the case of an undefended divorce, and by a High Court judge in the case of a defended divorce. An investigation will be carried out by a welfare officer whose report will guide the judge.

In Scotland, custody hearings will be in public before a sheriff in the sheriff court, or a judge in the Court of Session. If the sheriff or judge wants to see the children of the marriage, he will often do so in his own private chambers rather than in open court. A report by the local Social Services Department may be ordered by the sheriff or judge, usually in defended cases.

Child abduction

It is a criminal offence for a person to take or keep a child from the lawful custody of anyone entitled to it, without having the lawful authority of that person, or a reasonable excuse to do so. In cases in which one parent has been given custody of the child following divorce or lawful separation and the other parent unlawfully removes the child, the custodial parent may apply to the court to have the child returned.

A number of European countries have joined together to form the European Convention on the Custody of Children, which will ensure that if children are abducted from Britain to one of the countries which is a party of the agreement, they will try to discover the whereabouts of the child, and if necessary take court action to have the child returned.

If the child is taken to a country which is not part of the convention, it will be up to the custodial parent to take the necessary steps to find the child, at their own expense (see page 82 for Wardship Proceedings).

In Scotland, hearings will be in public before a sheriff in the sheriff court or a judge in the Court of Session. If the sheriff or judge wants to see the children of the marriage, he will often do so in his own private chambers rather than in open court.

4.7 Children

Birth

Normally it is a criminal offence for anyone other than a doctor or midwife to supervise a birth. In cases of emergency, however, the law recognises that an unqualified person may be called upon to deliver a child, and no action will be taken against that person provided that every effort was made to contact either a doctor, a midwife, or a hospital.

All births must be registered with the Registrar General. The following particulars are required:

(a) date and place of birth;
(b) name, surname and sex of child;
(c) name, surname, place of birth and occupation of father;
(d) name, surname, maiden name, place of birth and occupation of mother;
(e) mother's usual address if different from that of child's place of birth.

The birth must be registered within 42 days (in Scotland, twenty-one) by either one of the parents, and at this time a birth certificate will be issued.

Still born children also have to be registered.

A birth certificate may be needed to prove identity, age and citizenship, and in order to apply for a passport.

Contraception

Contraception is only legal when it actually prevents pregnancy – anything which is designed to act once pregnancy has occurred is not truly a contraceptive. The law does not define exactly when a woman becomes pregnant but it is generally taken to be some days after fertilisation when the fertilised egg implants into the womb. Therefore the IUCD and post coital contraception are still contraceptives not abortifacients.

Legally a doctor can give contraceptive advice to a child under 16 without the parents' consent, provided the child understands the advice given and its importance, and the doctor feels it is absolutely necessary.

Abortion – England and Wales only

It is a criminal offence for anyone to carry out an abortion on a woman who is (or believes she is) pregnant. However, in England and Wales only, it is permissible for a doctor to carry out an abortion where there is:

(a) a risk to the mother's life;
(b) a risk to the mother's mental or physical well being; or
(c) a risk that the child would be born with a physical or mental abnormality.

Two doctors must agree to the necessity for an abortion.

An abortion is only permissible if the foetus is incapable of being born alive (taken to be up to 28 weeks). In practice, few abortions are performed after 20 weeks.

Only doctors have the authority to perform the act of abortion. No nurse or doctor can be compelled to be party to an abortion unless there is a risk to the mother's life.

Abortions can be obtained either through the NHS or through private clinics, which may have charitable status and charge a small fee. The consent of the father is not necessary for an abortion.

Illegitimacy

The stigma attached to a child born out of wedlock has now been eliminated from the legal system by the Family Law Reform Act. Illegitimate children now have the same rights as those born within marriage, and references made to the legitimacy of children in legal documents have been abolished.

Adoption

A child can be adopted at any age between 19 weeks and 18 years. However, the child may be handed to the prospective adoptive parents from the age of six weeks. If the child is related to the adoptive parents or if it has been placed by an official adoption agency, the application for adoption can be made three months after the child has lived with them. In other cases, the child must live with the adoptive parents for 12 months before the application for adoption can be made to the court.

If the natural parents are married, both parents must consent to the adoption of their child. If they are unmarried, the consent of the father of the child is not necessary, although the court would be prepared to listen to his views. However, if the consent of the parent is unreasonably refused, his wishes may be ignored by the courts.

The requirements for adoption are very stringent; basically the prospective parents must be able to provide a happy and secure home for the child.

All adoptions must be arranged through an approved intermediary such as an adoption agency. There will be an adoption court hearing at which the person applying for the adoption must be present. If the child is of a suitable age it may also be required to attend the hearing in order to agree to the adoption.

On adoption, the child assumes the same legal rights as a natural child born to the adoptive parents.

Custodianship

Custodianship, which is something short of adoption but more than fostering, vests legal custody of a child in the applicant.

Before a custodianship order will be granted, the consent of the current legal guardian usually has to be obtained. The legal guardian may be a local authority, foster parents or a close relative. The granting of the order does not necessarily cut the ties between the child and the natural parents, but most of the parental rights and duties relating to the upbringing of the child are transferred to the custodian. There will be no rights to the estate or property of either party as a result of the order. Custodianship ceases either when the child reaches the age of 18, or if the order is revoked by the court.

Fostering

In many cases fostering is an alternative to adoption or care orders, particularly where the natural parents are experiencing temporary difficulties in coping with their children.

Fostering may be arranged either privately or through the local authority. If arranged privately, the local authority must be informed in advance if the proposed foster parent is *not* a relative or guardian of the child, and if the fostering is expected to last more than six days, so that they may check that the proposed foster home is suitable.

Wardship

If it is felt that a child under the age of 18 is in need of legal protection, it may be made a ward of court. Legal custody of the child is transferred to the court, which then has the right to make decisions which affect the well-being of the child. The court may delegate the responsibility of looking after the child to the local authority or some other suitable person.

Wardship proceedings are most often used in cases of emergency, such as where there is a possibility that the child may be kidnapped and taken abroad.

Parental obligations towards children

Parents are under a legal obligation to feed, clothe and properly provide for their children. Failure to do so can amount to a criminal offence. Children must receive full time education after their fifth birthday (although there are regional variations under this age). Compulsory education comes to an end at 16, the actual date of termination depending on the date of birth of the child.

Parents, guardians, foster parents and teachers are the only people who can lawfully punish a child, and the punishment must be fair and reasonable. Anyone else who punishes a child risks prosecution for assault.

Both parents whilst married are equally responsible for the upbringing of their children.

Parents have no right to withhold consent to essential medical treatment, whether this be on religious or moral grounds. The law allows a child of 16 and over to give consent to medical treatment; under 16 the law suggests that if a child is capable of fully understanding what medical treatment is being proposed, he or she can consent to it. Occasionally local authorities, through social workers, may seek to make a child a ward of court so that the necessary consent can be obtained.

How the law affects children

Parents incur no liability for any contracts entered into by their children under the age of 18, unless they have accepted such liability in writing. Normally a parent cannot be sued successfully for damage caused by a child, although they may be liable if it can be shown that they were in any way negligent, for example by lack of supervision. A child is responsible for his actions if he is old enough to be aware of their consequences – his youth is not always a defence. A child who is a victim of someone else's negligence can sue via his parent or guardian, known throughout the proceedings as his 'next friend'.

A child cannot be made to repay money he has borrowed unless he has spent the money on 'necessary' goods such as clothes and food. Similarly, if a minor receives goods on credit he cannot be made to pay for them.

In Scotland contracts made by minors (boys under 14 and girls under 12) are challengeable if made without their parents' or guardian's consent. If made with such consent, the contracts are generally valid.

Juvenile crime

The general term 'juvenile' refers to anyone under the age of 17. The law makes a distinction in this age group between people under the age of 14 ('children'), and those aged between 14 and 16 ('young persons').

Juveniles are regarded as a special case by the law, and courts must 'have regard to the welfare of the child or young person and shall in a proper case take steps for removing him from undesirable surroundings, and for seeing that proper provision is made for his education and training'.

Most cases against juveniles are brought in 'juvenile courts' which are magistrates' courts, with simpler procedures and less formality than normal adult courts. No members of the public are admitted to such hearings, and although the press are allowed to report, no mention must be made of the names of the juvenile defendants unless permission is granted by the court for them to do so. Any child who has reached the age of criminal responsibility (10 years) may be brought before a juvenile court. Anyone below the age of 10 may not be charged with any offence; between the ages of 10 and 13 inclusive, a juvenile is presumed not to understand that his actions are wrong, and in such cases it is up to the prosecution to prove that the juvenile did know that what he did was wrong in order to secure a conviction. After the age of 14, a juvenile may be convicted of a criminal offence in the same way as an adult, although the sentencing system is different.

In Scotland, the age of criminal responsibility can be any age at which the court is of the opinion that the child knew that what he was doing was wrong. Where the child is under seven, the question is determined by a Children's Panel.

Minimum age limits

Minimum age	Actions permitted by law
Birth	savings accounts may be opened on behalf of the child
6 weeks	may be handed to prospective adopters
19 weeks	may be formally adopted
2 years	may be sent to nursery school
3 years	can no longer travel free on public transport

5 years	must be sent for full time education; may drink alcohol in private
7 years	may withdraw money from Post Office
10 years	can be convicted of crime if it can be shown that they knew that it was wrong, except that in Scotland, in theory, there is no lower age limit for conviction or or sentencing
12 years	can buy a pet
13 years	may open a bank account at the discretion of the bank manager – will usually need someone to guarantee cheques
14 years	can take a part-time job; can be convicted of a criminal offence in the same way as an adult; may be fined up to £200 and sent to a detention centre; can own an airgun; can go into a bar with an adult, but cannot consume alcohol; a boy can be convicted of rape or unlawful intercourse with an under age girl; can have finger prints taken by police provided they have obtained a court order to do so (in Scotland, any age)
15 years	can own a shotgun and ammunition; can be sent to youth custody; can be admitted to film rated 15
16 years	can marry if they have received parental consent (in Scotland, parental consent is not necessary at this age); can apply for supplementary benefit (provided they have left full time education); can buy fireworks; can consent to medical treatment and choose own doctor; can leave school and take up full time employment; can join a trade union; can drink beer or cider in a pub, only with a meal in a part of the pub that serves meals and not at the bar; can drive a moped or tractor;

can buy cigarettes (can smoke at any age);
can pay for prescriptions;
can join the armed forces with parental consent (boy);
can consent to sexual intercourse (girls) (in Northern
Ireland the age of consent is 17)

17 years   can drive a motor vehicle (except HGV or PSV);
can enter a betting shop, but cannot bet;
can be tried on any charge in an adult court, and be sent
to prison;
can buy or hire a crossbow;

18 years   can vote;
can sue in their own name;
can marry without parental consent;
can change their name;
can apply for a passport;
can own land in own right;
can enter into binding contracts;
can obtain credit and have cheque/credit cards;
can be eligible for jury service;
can buy drinks in a bar;
can gamble;
can make a will (in Scotland 16);
can join the armed forces without parental consent;
can be admitted to a film rated 18;
can drive public service vehicle and medium heavy
goods vehicle

21 years   can drive heavy goods vehicle

Child abuse

All children have a right to legal protection against abuse of any sort – such
as assault, ill-treatment, neglect, sexual or emotional abuse. Anyone who
suspects that a child is being mistreated should make a report to the local
council social services department, the NSPCC or some other such organisation, following which there will be an investigation. A place of safety order
may be placed on the child by a magistrates' court if someone who suspects
abuse applies. This order will authorise the applicant to take the child to a
safe place for a maximum of 28 days. In serious cases, this may be followed
by a care order, placing the child in the care of the local authority. In such

cases all parental rights are transferred to the local authority. The care order will continue until the child is 18 or the order is discharged by the court.

Sexual intercourse with a close relative such as a daughter, son, or niece, is a criminal offence whatever the age of the party concerned. Intercourse with a child under 16 is assault, even if the child consents and realises what he or she is consenting to, and will amount to rape if the child does not consent or does not comprehend what he or she is consenting to. Incest is often repeated and known to at least one other member of the family. It is vital that help is sought for a victim of incest because a continuing situation can result in long term psychiatric or social problems.

Since 1967, anal intercourse (buggery) is no longer a criminal offence between consenting males over 21, but is still a punishable offence between a male and a female whether she consents or not.

4.8 Animals

Anyone who owns an animal is legally obliged to ensure that it does not cause damage to other people or their property. The owner must take all reasonable steps to make sure the animal cannot escape – he must not be negligent. If negligence is proved, then the owner of the animal will be liable for any damage or injury caused.

If the animal in question is of a dangerous species, as defined in the Dangerous Animals Act 1971 (one which is not usually domesticated in this country and is, when fully grown, likely to cause severe damage unless restrained), the owner will be strictly liable for any damage caused, no matter how many precautions he took to restrain the animal.

Strict liability will also apply if the animal is known by its owner to have a violent streak and causes damage or personal injury to another. Similarly, if the animals in question are livestock and they wander onto another person's property and cause damage, the owner must again accept the blame.

4.9 Medical Matters

Any medical examination is basically an assault at law. It is justified only by the informed consent of the patient. If the patient cannot give consent because of age or infirmity, then only necessary or emergency treatment can be given. The patient (this includes patients under 16 years of age) has a right to confidentiality from his doctor.

Hospital

In normal circumstances National Health Service hospitals will only accept patients referred to them by doctors, and even then such acceptance is subject to the availability of resources. No-one has the automatic right to hospital treatment, and cannot simply walk in off the street unless there is an emergency.

In less serious cases, patients may be treated by the hospital without actually being admitted (as an out-patient). If the necessary treatment requires admission to hospital, it is common for the patient to be put on a waiting list and to wait until he reaches the top of the list before being contacted by the hospital. Of course if the condition of the patient suddenly deteriorates, the waiting list may be abandoned and the patient may be brought in straight away.

Consent

Before any treatment may be carried out by a hospital the patient's consent needs to be obtained. This may be obtained by implication, in writing or orally. Treatment administered to a patient without his consent may constitute assault for which legal action may be taken.

Written consent is needed for surgery or other treatments in which there is an inevitable degree of risk, no matter how small. The patient (or the parent or guardian of a child patient) will be asked to sign a form which states the type of surgery or treatment to be carried out.

In certain cases, special forms of consent recommended by the Medical Defence Union will be used by the hospital.

A patient who refuses to give consent cannot be treated, even if the case is an emergency. However, a patient who is unconscious and cannot consent or refuse, may be treated, even if it is known that they would have refused had they been conscious. If possible the next of kin of such a patient should be asked to give consent, but if they refuse the doctor is still permitted to do what is necessary to save the patient's life. In the case of a child under 16 the withholding of consent by a parent to emergency (lifesaving) treatment on religious or moral grounds can be overridden by a doctor.

Discharge from hospital

Any patient has the right to discharge himself from hospital at any time unless they are there under the Mental Health Act (see below). If the patient leaves hospital before a doctor has given authority for him to do so, the patient will be asked to sign a form stating that he has left against the doctor's advice. This is a safeguard for the doctor should anything happen as a result of early discharge. If the patient refuses to sign the form, he cannot be prevented from leaving.

If the doctor gives his consent for the patient to be discharged, but it subsequently appears that the patient was not well enough to be discharged and he suffers as a result, he may sue the doctor for negligence. The doctor may also be sued if he fails to exercise reasonable skill and care towards the patient whilst in the hospital.

Doctors are under no obligation to treat a patient who is abusive or violent.

Complaints against a hospital

If you feel you have been injured as a result of the negligence of hospital staff, you may complain through the National Health Service's complaints procedure, by first of all writing to the administrator of the hospital concerned.

If you were a patient in a private hospital, there will not necessarily be a complaints procedure for you to follow. Whether or not you are happy with the treatment you receive in hospital, your insurers, if you are insured, will pay the doctors concerned – you will have little say in the matter. If you feel that negligence has occurred, you will have to take legal action, which will prove very costly. However, if you do wish to claim compensation for the injury you have suffered, you will have to obtain an independent medical opinion and seek legal advice from a solicitor who has expertise in this sort of litigation.

Your solicitor will have to gain access to your medical records from the hospital or doctor concerned, and hand them on to the independent medical advisor involved. If the hospital concerned refuses to co-operate, you may take legal action against them to ensure that they release the records.

When faced with a problem of this nature, you must be aware of the need to prove negligence. The fact that some sort of harm has come to you while in hospital is not enough – if you cannot prove that someone who owed you a duty of care acted negligently towards you, and injury has resulted from that action, you will have no grounds for compensation. The field of medical negligence is very difficult – accidents may occur for which no-one can be blamed.

Complaints against a GP

If you have a complaint against your GP, this should be made in the first instance to the Family Practitioner Committee, the local address being in the phone book. Doctors also have professional bodies which issue Codes of Practice to which they should adhere.

4.10 Mental Health

Mentally ill patients may have to be compulsorily detained for varying periods, if it is in their best interest, or the interest of others. They may be detained under various sections of the Mental Health Act.

An application may be made by the nearest relative, together with the written recommendation of two doctors. Emergency applications may be made by any relative or mental welfare officer, together with one doctor's recommendation. An order made following such an application is usually for 72 hours initially.

Some mentally ill patients have to be placed under guardianship if their families cannot care for them. Local authorities may act as guardians and there is a facility for patients to apply for a review or discharge of such guardianship to a Mental Health Tribunal. There are similar statutory provisions in Scotland.

The Court of Protection

Patients who lose legal capacity by reason of mental disorder and are unable to deal with their own financial affairs may have this responsibility transferred to a close relative, or if they have none, to the relevant local authority. Anyone who finds themselves in the position of having to look after such a person should make an application to the Court of Protection for a receiver to be appointed. In Scotland, the appropriate application to the Court is for the appointment of a *curator bonis*.

In such cases the patient must be served notice of the receivership. This may be done by the patient's own GP, who must certify that the action is necessary. The person appointed as receiver will be required to account annually to the court with regard to the income and outgoings of the estate, together with the necessary supporting evidence. If the patient recovers, the receivership does not automatically terminate; an application must be made to the Court of Protection.

Power of attorney

Normally, if a person who gives what is known as a general power of attorney authorising someone else to conduct legal affairs on his behalf, and the person giving the power later becomes incapable of managing their affairs (usually because of mental incapacity), that attorney must stop acting. However, since 10 March 1986 that need not necessarily apply provided, first, that the power of attorney was an 'enduring' one in a special form, and, second, that it was registered with the Court of Protection. This important development, which should be of particular use to families wanting to do the best for aged or infirm relatives, needs the early specialist advice and assistance of a solicitor to ensure the proper steps are taken.

4.11 Death

Deaths must be reported to the local registrar of Births Deaths and Marriages within five days of their occurrence (in Scotland eight days), and three certificates must be obtained:

(a) *medical certificate*, issued by the doctor in attendance stating the cause of death;
(b) *disposal certificate*, formal aproval for the body to be buried or cremated;
(c) *death certificate*, issued by the Registrar on production of the medical certificate.

The following particulars of the death are needed:

- date and place of death;
- name, surname and sex of the deceased;
- date and place of birth;
- occupation and usual address of the deceased;
- cause of death;
- name and surname, qualification, usual address and signature of informant;
- date of registration and the signature of the registrar.

Post mortem

If the death occurred in unusual or suspicious circumstances, the Coroner (or, in Scotland, the Procurator Fiscal) must be informed. He may feel it necessary to carry out a post mortem examination in order to establish the cause of death. A coroner is usually a doctor and may also be a lawyer, and it is his duty to order an investigation of all deaths which are sudden, accidental or suspicious, by means of a detailed medical examination of the body. Occasionally a post mortem will be ordered in the interests of medical research rather than to establish the cause of death, but this is very rare.

The responsibility for notifying the coroner of a death rests with the registrar who is under a duty to do so in the following circumstances:

(a) if the deceased was not being attended to by a doctor during the course of his last illness;
(b) if the proper documentation has not been produced;
(c) if the doctor who signed the certificate did not see the deceased after death, nor in the 14 days before death;

(d) if the cause of death is unknown;

(e) if the death was unnatural, or came about in suspicious circumstances;

(f) if the death occurred during an operation, or as the result of an anaesthetic;

(g) if death was due to industrial disease or industrial poisoning.

Inquest (in Scotland, fatal accident inquiry)

The Coroner or Procurator Fiscal may decide that an inquest (a public inquiry) into the death is necessary. This must be held if death was:

(a) violent or unnatural;

(b) sudden or inexplicable;

(c) in prison;

(d) in such circumstances as to constitute a risk to public health and safety.

The coroner must summon a jury (which must consist of between seven and eleven people) if the death occurred in prison or was in circumstances which constitute a public danger. On other occasions he may hear the case alone.

The body must be available for the inquest to take place, although exceptions to this are made where, for example, the body is known to have been destroyed. The inquest must be opened as soon as possible after the discovery of the body; if there are criminal proceedings in progress with regard to the death the inquest may be adjourned until they are over. The coroner also has the right to summon any witnesses who may be able to offer material evidence on the circumstances surrounding the death. Anyone who refuses to attend as a witness may be liable to imprisonment and/or a fine.

If the inquest has been heard by a jury they will be called upon to deliver a verdict on the death, upon which no more than two of the jurors can disagree. The usual verdicts given are:

(a) lawful killing, where the person who killed has an authority to do so, for example in cases of wartime hostilities;

(b) unlawful killing, ie murder or manslaughter. In Scotland, the equivalent concept is culpable homicide;

(c) suicide, where the person takes his own life;

(d) accidental, for example, a road accident;

(e) misadventure, where the dead person was partly at fault;

(f) death from industrial disease;

(g) natural, for example, a heart attack;

(h) open verdict, where there is not enough evidence upon which to base a verdict.

Each central police station has an officer known as 'the coroner's officer', who handles the procedural aspects of the inquest. Interested parties may choose to have legal representation especially if the verdict might have future repercussions, for example a claim of negligence. (This does not apply to Scotland.)

Human remains

The right to dispose of a corpse rests with the personal representatives. The body cannot at law be stolen, but its shrouds and coffin can be. There is no time limit for disposal of the body, nor a prescribed manner for disposal, but disposal must not cause a nuisance to the public or breach health regulations.

It is an offence, however, to conceal a corpse, destroy it to prevent an inquest, prevent its burial, or remove it from a grave without lawful authority.

The absence of a body, or any trace of it, does not prevent a charge of murder, but circumstantial evidence beyond a reasonable doubt will be necessary for a conviction.

Clinical or 'brain' death requires certification by two independent doctors one 24 hours after the other that there are no 'brain stem' responses.

Funerals

It is always advisable to make known to your family, both orally and in your will, any special requests concerning your funeral. Although the person(s) who arrange your funeral are under no legal obligation to follow any wishes you may have, if any special request has been made it is usually respected.

If you have to arrange a funeral, remember that many funeral directors belong to the National Association of Funeral Directors, which has drawn up a code of practice for its members to follow. Members must:

(a) offer a basic simple funeral service;
(b) give a written estimate of all funeral charges and an itemised invoice;
(c) ensure that advertising is clear, honest and in good taste;
(d) provide full and fair information about services and prices and offer guidance on certification and registration of death, social security benefits and the application of insurance policies in each case;
(e) provide speedy and sympathetic handling of complaints;
(f) provide suitable training for management in client relations;
(g) display the Association's symbol on the premises.

4.12 Wills, Probate and Intestacy

By leaving a will, you can direct what happens to your property, make provision for your family and dependents and appoint guardians for your children to assist a surviving spouse. The will must be drawn up and witnessed correctly, otherwise it may be invalid in whole or in part. This will result in your property being treated as if you had died intestate (without a will), and could mean that your estate is not distributed as you wish. In order to make a will you must be of sound mind and over 18 years of age (in Scotland 16 years of age). For a will to be valid it must, usually, be in writing, and signed or acknowledged by the testator/trix, in the presence of two witnesses present at the same time as each other. There are exceptions for the Armed Forces.

The property you own in your own right or have a share in, is your estate, and upon your death the only people entitled to deal with it are your personal representatives. Your personal representatives will be the 'executors' if there is a valid will, or 'administrators' if there is no will.

Challenging a will

Failure to make adequate financial provision for your spouse and dependants can lead to your will being disputed. If you choose to leave anyone out of your will, who would under normal circumstances expect to benefit, you should say why in the will or in a document left with it.

In Scotland, close relatives are entitled to specific proportions of a deceased's estate. However, if a will excluding such relatives is made, and is unchallenged, it may be administered in accordance with the decreased's wishes.

Challenges to a will must be made within six months from the date on which the court issues the grant of probate to the executors, or a grant of representation to the administrators. Either grant can be suspended following a successful application by aggrieved parties, who must be one of the following:

(a) spouse, including former spouses if the marriage has been dissolved for less than a year, and for whom no financial provision has yet been made; also former spouses who have not remarried;
(b) children, whether or not legitimate, or adopted or treated as being children of the deceased by the deceased;
(c) any other person who has been maintained by the deceased either wholly or partially prior to his death.

If the challenge is successful the applicant will be awarded a 'reasonable financial provision' out of the proceeds of the estate.

In Scotland, a will will be valid if completely written in the handwriting of the testator and signed by the testator. A will written by someone else, or printed or typed, will be valid if the words 'adopted as holograph' are added by the testator, who then signs. In each of these types of will, no witnesses are required.

There is no need to use a solicitor for drawing up a will, but it is generally advisable. You must ensure that everything in the will is precise and not open to numerous interpretations. You must also select the executors to the will, generally two people who may or may not benefit from your will, who will be responsible for ensuring that your wishes and instructions are carried out. No-one who benefits under the will, or who is related to any such beneficiary, should witness the testator's signature. Executors *can* act as witnesses if they do not benefit, but it is advisable for them not to do so.

Once the will has been signed and witnessed, any subsequent changes must be incorporated either in a new will, which will revoke the old one, or in the case of smaller changes, in a codicil, which is a supplement to the will and may add to or change clauses in the earlier will. The formalities for the completion of a codicil are identical to that of the will. In theory there is no limit to the number of codicils which may be made to a will, but it is preferable to keep the number as low as possible to avoid complications. If substantial changes have to be made, then a new will should be drafted.

There are a number of grounds upon which the validity and content of a will can be challenged, for example:

- authenticity of the signatures;
- testator's ability to fully understand the implications of the will;
- interpretation of the will.

The effect of marriage and divorce on the will

Under provisions contained in the wills Act, if the testator fails to make a new will after marriage, he will die intestate, since the act of marriage revokes all previous wills (except in Scotland), unless made in contemplation of the marriage. If this is the case, it should be clearly stated in the will.

Unless there are provisions to the contrary, divorce will eliminate the ex-spouse from the existing will. Thus if the testator states that the ex-spouse should still benefit from the estate despite the divorce, then the ex-spouse will remain entitled. However, if the testator subsequently re-marries then the existing will will be invalidated and the ex-spouse will lose the entitlement. Upon re-marriage, if the ex-spouse is to benefit, it is essential to make a new will.

Obtaining a grant

If the estate is small or simple, and especially if the deceased is survived by a spouse with whom he owned everything jointly, it may be unnecessary to obtain a grant of probate or letters of administration from the court. Circulation of the death certificate may suffice to provide evidence of death and the capacity of the personal representative to administer the estate.

No grant will be required if there is no land among the assets of the estate, but only money contained in bank or building society accounts, amounting to no more than £5,000.

Grants can be applied for without recourse to solicitors, ie 'personally', and forms are available from the Principal or any District or sub Probate Registry. The usual papers required are a sworn document (affidavit), the will and codicils (if applicable), an an Inland Revenue form and court fees. In all but the simplest of cases it is advisable to consult a solicitor, whose fees will come out of the estate.

Remember: (i) Executors can decide not to accept their appointment and 'renounce' it;

(ii) anyone wishing to challenge issue of a grant to a will or an intestate estate can file a 'caveat' to prevent the grant being issued (see below);

(iii) anyone can search for an issued grant at the Principal Registry and obtain a copy.

A caveat is really a warning, usually in the form of an entry in the Register, which is intended to prevent the issuing of the grant of probate without the person making the entry being informed.

Intestacy

If you do not make a will your property will be divided in accordance with provisions contained in the Administration of Estates Act:

(a) if you are married and have no children your spouse will inherit the first £125,000 of your estate and all your personal possessions;

(b) if you are married and have children your spouse will inherit the first £75,000 of your estate and your personal possessions, and any remaining property is divided equally among the children, but your spouse will have a life interest in half of this remainder;

(c) if you have no spouse but you do have children your estate will be divided equally among them;

(d) if you have no spouse or children, your parents will inherit everything;

(e) if you have no parents, your spouse, children or nearest blood relatives will inherit.

Personal representatives (executors or administrators)

The first duty of personal representatives is to provide for the burial or cremation of the deceased. Thereafter, they collect in the assets of the estate, discharge all valid debts, issue or receive court proceedings on behalf of the estate and discharge any death duties and other taxes. Finally the estate is distributed by the personal representatives either in accordance with the will or if there is none or it is defective, by applying the rules of intestate succession. These rules are complex and there are financial thresholds which are increased periodically.

An important difference between executors of wills and administrators of estates where there was no valid will (all generally called 'personal representatives') is that the right to administer the estate for executors starts immediately on the death of the testator, whereas administrators need the grant of letters of administration to give them authority to act.

With regard to intestacy in Scotland, you would be advised to consult your local sheriff clerk's department or to see your solicitor who will advise.

Inheritance Tax

This has recently replaced Capital Transfer Tax (which itself replaced the old Estate Duty), and in its simplest form, deals with lifetime transfers of gifts.

This area of the law is extremely complex and the advice of a solicitor or an accountant should be sought when dealing with it. Generally, if the deceased lived in the UK, then all of his estate, wherever situated, is considered potentially taxable. If a deceased did not live in the UK at the time of death, only UK assets are taxable. After deductions such as outstanding debts, liabilities and funeral expenses, the net estate is taxed.

Certain property is excluded from the estate, and certain 'transfers' are exempt, principally all property, whatever the value, going to a surviving spouse. Some property is given special treatment with percentage reductions in tax (eg business property) or value (eg farm land).

In Scotland, the position regarding death duty and deeds of family arrangement is similar, but again the law is highly complex and the advice of a solicitor or accountant should be sought.

4.13 Contact Points

Child abuse

Childline: Tel: 0800 1111
A charitable helpline for victims of abuse

Incest Crisis Line Main Offices:
(will give local contacts)

66 Marriott Close
Bedfont
Feltham
Middlesex
Tel: (01) 890 4732

Provides help and advice for victims of incest.

National Society for the Prevention of Cruelty to Children. (NSPCC)
67 Saffron Hill
London EC1N 8RS
Tel: (01) 242 1626

Will investigate complaints reported to them; gives information and advice on child abuse. Local offices throughout the country.

Royal Scottish Society for the Prevention of Cruelty to Children
Melville House
41 Polwarth Terrace
Edinburgh EH11 1NU
Tel: (031) 337 8539

Child Poverty Action Group
1–5 Bath Street
London EC1V 9PY
Tel: (01) 253 3406

Publishing and campaigning body concerned with issues affecting families and parents.

Advisory and support groups

The Organisation for Parents Under Stress (OPUS)
106 Godstone Road
Whyteleafe
Surrey CR3 OEB
Tel: (01) 645 0469

Advises and assists parents who are experiencing difficulties with family relationships. Also co-ordinates support groups with telephone advice being given by trained volunteer parents.

National Association of Young Peoples Counselling and Advisory Services
(NAYPCAS)
17–23 Albion Street
Leicester LE1 6GD
Tel: (0533) 471200

Advises and counsels young people experiencing difficulties in family
relationships.

Rape Crisis Line
PO Box 46
Belfast BT7 1RL
Tel: (0232) 249696

Provides help and advice for victims of rape and information on local support
groups.

Rape Crisis Centre
PO Box 69
London WC1X 9NJ
Tel: (01) 837 1600

Rape Crisis Centre
PO Box 120
Edinburgh EH1 3ND
Tel: (031) 556 9437

Rape Crisis Centre
PO Box 53
Glasgow G2 1YR
Tel: (041) 221 8448

British Association for Counselling
37a Sheep Street
Rugby
Warwickshire CV21 3BX
Tel: (0788) 78328

Provides counselling and support for anyone who feels that they need it.

National Childrens Bureau
8 Wakely Street

London EC1V 7QE

Tel: (01) 278 9441

Promotes and safeguards the interests of children. Offers lists of organisations concerned with the problems of young people, and various aspects of family relationships, including juvenile crime, delinquency, education and adoption.

National Association for the Welfare of Children in Hospital
Argyle House
29/31 Euston Road
London NW1 2SD
Tel: (01) 833 2041

Offers help and support to parents before, during and after their child's stay in hospital.

National Council for One Parent Families
255 Kentish Town Road
London NW5 2LX
Tel: (01) 267 1361

Offers free and confidential help to parents-to-be and single pregnant women.

Gingerbread
35 Wellington Street
London WC2E 7BN
Tel: (01) 240 0953

Scottish Gingerbread
39 Hope Street
Glasgow G3 7DW
Tel: (041) 248 6840

National self-help associations for one parent families with local groups throughout the country where lone parents meet other people who are also bringing up children alone.

Families Need Fathers
39 Cloonmore Avenue
Orpington
Kent BR6 9LE
Tel: (0689) 54343

A society which campaigns for equal parental rights, and provides counselling and advice for both parents going through separation and divorce.

Childrens Legal Centre
20 Compton Terrace
London N1 2UN
Tel: (01) 359 6251

An independent body concerned with laws and policies which affect children and young people in England and Wales. It provides free advice and information by telephone and letter.

Justice for Children
35 Wellington Street
London WC2E 7BN
Tel: (01) 836 5917

Offers advice on issues relating to the child care system and procedures.

National Foster Care Association
Francis House
Francis Street
London SW1P 1DE
Tel: (01) 826 6266

Institute for the Study of Drug Dependence
1–4 Hatton Place
(off St. Cross St.)
Hatton Garden
London EC1N 8ND
Tel: (01) 430 1991

Publishes information on the non-medical use of drugs. Provides information about volunteer groups offering support and other sources of information and advice for parents of drug users.

Drugline
9A Brockley Cross
London SE4 2AB
Tel: (01) 692 4975

Advice and support services.

Advisory Centre for Education
18 Victoria Park Square
London E2 9PB
Tel: (01) 980 4596

Offers free advice to parents with children at state schools. Publishes a bi-monthly bulletin for anyone concerned with education.

Education Otherwise
25 Common Lane
Hemmingford Abbotts
Cambs PE18 9AN
Tel: (0480) 63130

Self-help organization offering support, advice and information to families practising or contemplating home-based education as an alternative to schooling.

Independent School Information Service
56 Buckingham Gate
London SW1E 6AG
Tel: (01) 630 8793

Offers information and advice to parents on behalf of the leading associations of independent schools.

Solicitors' Family Law Association
154 Fleet Street
London EC4A 2HX
Tel: (01) 353 3290

Association of matrimonial lawyers who subscribe to a code of practice designed to encourage and assist parties to reconcile differences. List of members is available from the secretary.

National Step Family Association
162 Tenison Road
Cambridge CB1 2DP
Tel: (0223) 460312

Offers practical help, support, information and advice to all members of step families and liaison with all those working with step families in a professional, voluntary or academic capacity. The Association puts members in touch with one another where desired and provides access to publications on the problems of step families. Also a telephone advice service.

Family Rights Group
6 Manor Gardens
Holloway Road

London N7 6LA
Tel: (01) 272 7308

Campaigns for the improvement of the law and practice relating to children
in care. Has a social worker and a solicitor who work with and for the parents.

National Association of Young People in Care
Maranar House
28/30 Mosley Street
Newcastle upon Tyne NE IDF
Tel: (091) 261 2178

An organization run by and for young people in care or who have been in
care, with the aim of improving conditions for them and helping to start
support groups. Also provides help and support.

Marriage breakdown

Marriage Guidance Council – local addresses to be found in phone book.

National Family Conciliation Council
34 Milton Road
Swindon SN1 5JA
Tel: (0793) 618486

(National headquarters). Will act as mediator between parties in order to sort
out ancillary matters – such as child custody and divorce.

Scottish Family Conciliation Council
1 Melrose Street
Glasgow G4 9EJ
Tel: (041) 332 2731

Adoption

British Agencies for Adoption and Fostering
11 Southwark Street   23 Castle Street
London SE1 1RQ   Edinburgh EH2 3DN
Tel: (01) 407 8800   Tel: (031) 225 9285

Produces leaflets and publications on adoption including a list of adoption
agencies throughout the country.

Parents for Children
222 Camden High Street
London NW1 8QR
Tel: (01) 485 7526

Helps to find adoptive homes for 'difficult' children.

Parent to Parent Information on Adoption Services
Lower Boddington
Daventry
Northants NN11 6YB
Tel: (0327) 60295

Puts existing and prospective adoptive parents in touch with each other to provide help and support nationwide. Also produces regular newsletter with details on children waiting for adoption.

Scottish Adoption Advice Centre
21 Castle Street   21 Elmbank Street
Edinburgh EH2 3DN   Glasgow G2 4TV
Tel: (031) 225 3666   Tel: (041) 339 0772

Mental health

The Court of Protection
25 Store Street
London WC1E 7BP
Tel: (01) 636 6877

Protects and administers the property and affairs of people who are incapable of so doing due to mental disability.

MIND (National Association of Mental Health)
22 Harley Street
London W1N 2ED
Tel: (01) 637 0741

Provides information, advice and assistance on any matter relating to mental health, law and policy; also provides free representation before a Mental Health Review Tribunal.

Scottish Association for Mental Health
40 Shandwick Place
Edinburgh EH2 4RR

Tel: (031) 225 4446

Similar service to MIND

Northern Ireland Association for Mental Health
84 University Street
Belfast BT7 1HE
Tel: (0232) 228 474

Similar service to MIND.

Somerset House

Principal Registry of the Family Division
Somerset House
Strand
London WC2R 1LP
Tel: (01) 936 6000

Wills may be deposited at the Registry.

General Register Office
St Catherines House
10 Kingsway
London WC2B 6JP
Tel: (01) 242 0262

Registrar General for Births, Deaths and Marriages (will give local addresses).

Health and Welfare Organisations

Action for the Victims of Medical Accidents
24 Southwark Street
London SE1 1TY
Tel: (01) 403 4744

A registered charity which offers help and advice to victims of medical accidents.

Health Service Commissioner (Ombudsman)
Church House
Great Smith Street
London SW1P 3PW
Tel: (01) 212 7676

Investigates complaints about poor service and maladministration.

British Medical Association
BMA House   BMA – Scotland
Tavistock Square   7 Drumsheugh Gardens
London WC1H 9JP   Edinburgh EH3 7QP
Tel: (01) 387 4499   Tel: (031) 225 7184

BMA – Wales   BMA – Northern Ireland
195 Newport Road   609 Ormeau Road
Cardiff CF2 1UE   Belfast BT7 3JD
Tel: (0222) 485336   Tel: (0232) 649065

The professional body for doctors – will investigate complaints.

General Medical Council
44 Hallam Street
London W1N 6AE
Tel: (01) 580 7642

Governing body for the medical profession, which ensures that high standards of training and practice are met by the members. Will also investigate complaints of gross or serious malpractice and has its own disciplinary procedures.

General Dental Council
37 Wimpole Street
London W1M 8DQ
Tel: (01) 486 2172

Governing body for the dentistry profession. Has disciplinary powers, and will investigate serious complaints of malpractice against dentists on behalf of clients. Has the ultimate sanction of removing serious offenders from the register.

Association of Carers
21–23 New Road
Chatham
Kent ME4 4QJ
Tel: (0634) 813981

Offer advice, support and opportunities for self-help to carers for the disabled and/or elderly.

Age Concern
60 Pitcairn Road
Mitcham
Surrey CR4 3LL
Tel: (01) 640 5431

Information, research and training aimed at promoting the welfare of the elderly.

Disability Alliance
25 Denmark Street
London WC2H 8NJ
Tel: (01) 240 0806

Pressure group to pursue payment of regular income to the disabled.

National Association of Funderal Directors
57 Doughty Street
London WC1N 2NE
Tel: (01) 242 9388

Trade association which has a code of practice for members describing the type of service that should be offered.

PAIN
Parents Against Injustice
Plegdon Green
Nr Henman
Bishops Storford
Herts
Tel: (0279) 850549

Capital Taxes Office:
Minford House
Rockley Road
London W14 0DF
(01) 603 4622

Inland Revenue Stamp Duty Office
West Block
Barrington Rd, Worthing
West Sussex BN12 4XH
Tel: (0903) 502525.

5. Consumer Affairs

Great advances have been made in recent years in the protection given by the law to consumers, and the community is more and more aware of consumer rights. These are examined next.

5.1 Buying Goods

Whether you are purchasing goods or services, you are protected by a variety of consumer laws. The most important of these is the law of contract, but protection is also offered by the criminal law and the law of negligence.

When you enter a shop for the purpose of buying goods, you are making an offer to the shopkeeper to buy his goods. The shopkeeper may accept or reject your offer, but if he accepts and there is agreement on the price, a contract exists between you and the shopkeeper. This contract is enforceable at law. Implied in this contract between you and the shopkeeper are additional safeguards with regard to the quality and condition of the goods. These implied terms are contained in the Sale of Goods Act, and are:

(a) *Title*: the seller of goods must have the legal right to sell them.
(b) *Description*: goods sold must correspond exactly with the description offered by the seller. If they do not you will have the right to reject them.
(c) *Quality and fitness*: the goods sold must firstly be of merchantable (reasonable) quality, unless any defects have specifically been drawn to your attention prior to the sale. Secondly the goods must be reasonably fit for the purpose for which they have been supplied. If you ask the seller for advice on goods which you require for a specific purpose, and you rely on that purpose, then you have the right to return them and get a refund.

Rights and remedies

If you have any complaints, you should go to the seller of the goods with that complaint, and not to the manufacturer. Your contract is with the seller.

Remedies for the seller's breach of the contract under the Sale of Goods Act are:

(a) *Damages* – the effect being to compensate you and to put you in the same position as if the contract had been properly performed.
(b) *Rejection of the goods* – to be effective, the rejection must be made as soon as possible (ideally before the goods have been used). Such rejection will result in the purchase price being refunded.

A trader is prevented from unreasonably excluding liability for the implied conditions under the Sale of Goods Act, by provisions in the Unfair Contract Terms Act (see below).

You will lose your rights if:

(a) you examined the goods prior to purchase, and the faults were so obvious that you should have noticed them;
(b) the seller pointed out the faults in the items purchased before the sale was completed;
(c) you ignored the seller's skill or judgement as to the suitability of the goods for the purpose you described to him;
(d) the seller told you that he should not be relied upon as an expert, but nevertheless you still went ahead on the purchase;
(e) you have simply changed your mind about the item. Unless there is something wrong with the goods, the shop is under no duty to refund your money, although many do so as a goodwill gesture;
(f) you received the goods as a gift – the buyer is the one who made the contract and who should therefore make the complaint.

Remember: if you see a sign in a shop stating that no refunds are given (which is often the case with sale goods), it has no effect on your statutory rights, and the seller will be liable if he sells faulty goods or in some other way contravenes the sale of goods legislation.

When buying second hand or sale goods, although you still have the protection of the consumer legislation, the court will not expect the goods to be of the same standard as new goods.

Sunday trading is illegal (maximum fine £500) but many exceptions and anomalies exist. New legislation is expected.

5.2 Buying Services

Anyone who provides a service as opposed to selling goods, such as a plumber, surveyor or other professional, must do so with reasonable care and skill, in a reasonable length of time and for a reasonable charge. The Supply of Goods and Services Act imposes these conditions on any contract for the supplying of services. In addition, any goods supplied under such a contract must comply with the requirements above under the Sale of Goods Act.

If any dispute arises you should first complain to the person involved, then write a letter to the head office of the organisation concerned telling them of your complaint, and asking for a refund. The firm may belong to a trade association or professional body, and they may be able to help you settle the dispute by arbitration. As a last resort it may be necessary to take the matter to court.

5.3 Unfair Contract Terms Act

The purpose of this Act is to ensure that a trader does not try to impose 'unfair' conditions into a contract made between himself and a consumer. In particular, the Act totally prohibits the trader from trying to exclude liability for death or bodily injury caused by his negligence, and any attempt on his part to do so is illegal. Attempts made by the trader to exclude liability for other loss or damage must be reasonable. In all cases the trader must place notices stating that he wishes to exclude liability so that the consumers with whom he is dealing have adequate warning that such a clause is in operation.

Remember: If a shop displays a sign saying 'no responsibility accepted for loss or damage however caused', such an exclusion may not be valid.

The Act operates only for the protection of consumers in contracts made with traders, and does not operate in contracts made between private individuals. If a particular term of a contract is disputed and is subsequently found to be unfair by the court, it will be struck out of the contract.

5.4 Private Sales

If you buy privately your rights under the Sale of Goods Act are limited.

The private seller is still under an obligation to provide goods which are as described. If the goods are faulty and do not correspond with the seller's description, your main remedies (damages and/or rescission) may lie under the Misrepresentation Act. In certain circumstances it is difficult to distinguish between a private seller and a trader, for example if people are selling from home. If you are unsure of the capacity in which a person is dealing make sure you find out before you make the contract.

Remember: It is a criminal offence for a person to pretend they are selling as a private individual, when in fact they are a trader.

5.5 Buying at Auctions

Beware of auction sales. An auctioneer does not owe the same duty to you as a trader, so it is up to you to examine the goods before you start bidding to make sure they are what you want. In an auction, the auctioneer is inviting offers from bidders which he is free to accept or reject. If the offer is accepted by the auctioneer, no contract is made until the hammer drops. At this point neither party can back out of the contract.

5.6 Doorstep Sales

Although you have the same consumer rights when buying from a doorstep sales person you must exercise caution. Do not alow yourself to be pressurised into making a purchase, always satisfy yourself as to the credentials of the seller, and make a note of the firm's name and address. If you are purchasing goods on credit, special rules apply to doorstep sales (see credit sales, page 116).

5.7 Deposits

When you pay a deposit for goods which are not yet in stock, or for goods which are to be specially made to your requirements, you are making a binding contract with the trader, and you risk losing the deposit if you subsequently change your mind about wanting the goods. The trader is entitled to recover the full cost of the goods if you do change your mind.

5.8 Unsolicited Goods and Services

If you are sent goods through the post which you have not ordered, they become your property if the sender does not claim them back within six months. If you choose to write to the sender stating that the goods were unsolicited, he must collect them within 30 days or the goods will become your property.

5.9 Buying by Post

This is one of the most convenient methods of shopping, and usually takes one of the following forms:

- mail order through a catalogue company;
- buying from advertisements in publications – for example books and records.

Most firms allow you to have goods on approval for a specified length of time before they expect payment. Payment is usually offered on credit terms, and the credit may prove to be expensive. Many of the large mail order firms belong to the Mail Order Traders' Association, which has produced a Code of Practice. The Code of Practice states that:

(a) information about the goods must be stated clearly and accurately;
(b) failure to meet quoted delivery dates will give the customer the option to cancel the order and obtain a full refund;
(c) goods which turn out to be unsuitable or faulty can be returned with full refund;
(d) if the firm sends you substitute goods, those you order being unavailable, you have the right to return them if they are not suitable;
(e) the complaints procedure which is operated by the member should be simple and straightforward.

The Association of Mail Order Publishers is responsible for the Code of Practice relating to the purchase of books and records through the post. This code ensures that the advertisement clarifies the main terms and conditions of the offer; information about the goods on offer is given precisely; and if postage and packing are additional, this must be stated clearly.

5.10 Consumer Complaints

Whether your complaint concerns faulty goods or poor quality workmanship, there is a standard approach to making a successful complaint.

It is always advisable to keep receipts for a while after the purchase. It will make life a great deal easier for you if you can go back to a trader with a receipt, although it is not necessary to produce one to enforce your rights.

As soon as you become aware of the fault, you should stop using the goods in question immediately, and contact the trader, preferably in person. The reason for the urgency is that you may forfeit the right to demand your money back if you do not act promptly.

Remember: Your remedy lies with the retailer and not with the manufacturer when dealing with faulty goods.

Be polite but firm when making your complaint and point out the source of your dissatisfaction.

Always take the goods back in person if you can, and ask for the manager. In the case of services, take your complaint initially to the person who performed the service. This may be enough to settle the dispute. If you do not get the issue settled, you should write to the head office of the company concerned, demanding a solution.

Arbitration

Your next step will be to approach the relevant trade association, professional and consultative body (if the company concerned is a member of one). Such bodies will investigate complaints on your behalf and some offer arbitration services to settle disputes.

All arbitration schemes are administered by the Chartered Institute of Arbitrators. The scheme is intended to be a simple and inexpensive way of settling disputes between the consumer and the trader. The arbitrator decides the case on written evidence sent in by the consumer and the trader; very occasionally, a local hearing may be necessary but there is no extra cost for this.

The arbitrator normally takes about two weeks to reach a decision; he then makes his award which is final and legally binding on both parties, and must be paid within 21 days.

Going to court

If all else fails you can sue for the return of your money or compensation in the county court. There is a simple, low-cost, do-it-yourself system known as the Small Claims Court.

These claims will be heard by an arbitrator, who is generally a court registrar. The amount claimed must be no more than £500. Each side will have to pay their own legal costs; the reason for this is to discourage the use of solicitors in such claims where the legal costs could exceed the amount in dispute. The necessary forms are available from your local county court.

Anything over £500 will not be dealt with by the small claims procedure, except by consent of both parties.

In Scotland the equivalent of the small claims court is the summary cause court, which is presided over in the first instance by the sheriff clerk and, depending on the type of action, by a sheriff. Cases may be brought where the value of the claim is less than £1,000, and court expenses will normally be awarded to the successful party, but each party must meet any other costs, including their own solicitor's fees.

In Northern Ireland, the small claims court can hear claims up to the value of £300; if a claim is for more than this amount, then it is either heard by a circuit registrar or a county court judge depending on the amount being claimed.

Remedies

Exactly what you are entitled to when complaining about goods or services, depends on how serious the fault is and how soon you inform the trader:

Goods

- you may be entitled to reject the goods and get your money back; or
- be given a replacement or free repair; or
- get a cash payment to make up the difference between what you paid and the reduced value of the faulty items.

Services

- you may reduce the cost of the bill for the service; or
- you may have the service performed again; or
- you may be given your money back to go elsewhere for the service.

Who can help?

A number of organisations have been established to deal specifically with complaints:

(a) *Environmental Health Departments* deal with health matters including unfit food and drink and the hygiene standards of shops, restaurants and other catering establishments.
(b) Your local *Trading Standards Office* will investigate inaccurate weights and measures, the safety standards of particular goods, and false descriptions of prices.
(c) *Consumer Consultative Councils* deal with complaints against most public services such as British Rail, and the electricity boards.
(d) Complaints concerning maladministration by local authorities may be investigated by your local *Ombudsman*. Complaints against government departments may be dealt with by the Parliamentary Ombudsman.
(e) *Professional bodies* and *trade associations* will investigate complaints against members.

5.11 Banking

Banks offer a wide range of services which assist in handling your finances. When you open an account with a bank you enter into a formal contract with the bank, which consists of two parts:

(a) the bank undertakes to carry out your instructions by honouring cheques when they are presented for payment, provided that there is enough money in the account to do so;

(b) with limited exceptions, the bank owes you a duty of confidentiality, and cannot divulge any information to anyone without your permission.

If you have written a cheque which you later wish to stop, you may instruct the bank to withold payment on the cheque. If the bank fails to stop such a cheque, they must bear the loss. The act of stopping a cheque does not alter your liability to the person in whose favour it was drawn. If the cheque in question has been endorsed with your cheque card number, you may not stop it, since the card number acts as a guarantee that the payment will be met.

Unless you have previously negotiated an overdraft with the bank, they do not have to pay cheques which bring the account overdrawn. In such cases the cheque will be returned to the payee, marked 'R/D' (refer to drawer).

If your signature has been forged on a cheque, the banks should spot it and refuse to pay. However, if the signature is very similar to your own, the bank may not be liable for any losses, since it is up to the customer to notify the bank that cheques have gone missing.

When paying by cheque for goods, particularly those purchased through the post, it is advisable to cross the cheque so that if it is lost or stolen, it cannot be cashed – a crossed cheque can only be paid into a bank account. An uncrossed cheque may be presented over the counter of the bank branch on which it is drawn. As an additional safeguard, banks commonly issue their customers with cheques which are pre-crossed.

If a cheque is crossed 'not negotiable', it means that it cannot be endorsed and passed on as payment to someone else by the payee. If the cheque is crossed 'account payee', it acts as an instruction to the banker to credit the cheque to the payee's account and to no-one else's.

Remember: When writing a cheque:
- never sign a blank cheque;
- always take care to ensure that the amount of the cheque is written in in words commencing under the word 'pay', and leave the minimum amount of space between words;
- when writing the amount in figures in the box provided, do so in such a way as to ensure that the amount cannot

be altered;
- always initial any changes you make to a cheque; if you write out a new one, tear the old one up;
- *never* keep your cheque guarantee card with your cheque book.

5.12 Credit

The process of buying now and paying later is much in evidence in today's commercial world. Most of us have or will have at some stage, some sort of agreement with a credit company for goods which we would probably not be able to afford otherwise.

Credit cards

The most common type of credit facility used today is the credit card, such as Access and Visa. These enable the consumer to purchase a variety of goods in stores which accept credit cards, up to a specified credit allowance. Each month the consumer will receive a statement giving the details of the sales recorded during the previous month, the amount due, and the date on which the payment will be expected. The card holder has the option of paying a specified minimum amount of the sum due, but will incur interest on any balance outstanding. If the full sum is met when required, no interest will be charged. Thus, the consumer has the opportunity of obtaining interest-free credit for a number of weeks. When a trader accepts a credit card in payment for goods, he has to pay the credit card company a small percentage in commission.

The consumer is not responsible for the credit card until he has signed it. Even then the owner of the card will not be liable for any transactions above £50 which take place on the card without his knowledge or consent. If the card is lost or stolen, the owner will be liable for no more than this amount, unless he actually gave the card to the person who mis-used it. In any event you must report any loss to the credit card company as soon as possible.

When goods are purchased with a credit card, the purchaser has rights against the credit card company as well as the seller if the goods turn out to be faulty, provided they cost over £100. You should first of all try to settle the dispute with the seller, but if this not possible you are entitled to sue either the seller or the credit company for your loss.

Hire purchase and credit sales

Customers are not usually given a choice as to whether the agreement they enter into when purchasing an item on credit is on HP or credit sale, since most retailers have arrangements with a finance company which dictate the type of credit offered. Credit sale is becoming more common, since, if the buyer fails to make all the payments, it is easier for the finance company concerned to recover payments due from the customer through the courts, than to repossess the goods.

Remember: When goods are purchased under a hire purchase agreement, you do not own the goods until all the HP instalments have been paid; with a credit sale agreement, the ownership of the goods passes as soon as you take possession of them, and before the full purchase price has been paid.

In normal circumstances you are unable to back out of the credit agreement once it has been signed. However, if the agreement has not yet been finalised, (for example if the finance company has not formally agreed to provide the credit), it will be possible for you to withdraw from the agreement. If the agreement was signed 'off trade premises' (for example in your home), then the following procedure must be complied with by the trader (and failure by the trader to comply with the conditions will give the consumer the right to back out of the agreement):

(a) the trader must leave a copy of the signed agreement with you at the time the sale is made;

(b) a further copy of the agreement must be sent to you within seven days of the transaction;

(c) if within five days of receiving the second document you decide to back out of the agreement, you are entitled to do so. This five day period is known as the 'cooling off' period.

If you do decide to back out within this time, you must inform the seller within the stated time limit, by letter.

If you fall into arrears with HP payments, the finance company will only be able to repossess the goods with a court order in specific circumstances (see page 30). If you fall into arrears with the payments under a credit sale agreement, the seller can start legal proceedings against you to recover the loan. They cannot recover the goods since ownership in them has passed to you.

Where goods are unsatisfactory or faulty, the shopkeeper is liable in the same way as if the goods were purchased outright and not on credit. The finance company is also liable, so you will be able to take legal action against either the seller or the finance company. This gives you additional protection as the 'joint liability' is not restricted to goods bought on credit or HP, but applies to all credit purchases. It does not, however, apply to goods bought on a normal bank overdraft (see below).

Bank overdrafts and loans

Another method of obtaining credit is by means of a bank overdraft, which must usually be arranged in advance, and is charged at a rate of interest higher than the bank's 'base rate'. One disadvantage of this facility is that in addition to the interest charged on the amount of credit received by the customer, bank charges will be incurred on cheques presented and services provided during the time the account is overdrawn.

Banks also offer personal loans to customers, which will normally be a loan of a fixed amount, for a specified purpose (for example the purchase of a car), to be paid back in instalments over a specified period and usually wth a fixed rate of interest. The loan is usually set up in a separate account, so the customer need not incur further bank charges. The borrower's current account is usually automatically debited on a monthly basis with the repayments often compromising a mixture of interest and capital. A building society loan may be an alternative.

5.13 Consumer Safety

Safety standards

Legislation exists to ensure that certain safety standards are maintained in the manufacture and marketing of specific goods. Goods that are subject to these regulations fall into three broad categories:

- those which are dangerous to children;
- those which are poisonous;
- those which are capable of igniting or administering electric shocks.

The legislation lays down a number of measures which manufacturers must observe in order to ensure that goods are of a safe standard:

(a) they must regulate the composition, content, design, construction, finish and packaging of goods;
(b) they must ensure that the goods they produce come up to a particular standard. This standard will normally depend upon the type of goods being produced, and may be already established by some other body, such as the British Standards Authority;
(c) they must ensure that their goods are regularly tested and inspected.

Consumer safety is the prime concern of the legislation, and the goods to which it applies have to carry warnings and instructions about how to use them, and what to do in the case of accidents. Before any regulations can be imposed on manufacturers or suppliers, they must be consulted through their trade associations, as to the contents of the regulations to be imposed.

If manufacturers or suppliers contravene the safety legislation they may be fined and/or imprisoned. However, if it can be shown that all reasonable steps had been taken to observe the regulations imposed, this may be a valid defence. The responsibility for enforcing the safety regulations lies with the Trading Standards Department of the local authority.

Food

Most regulations concerning the production, handling and marketing of food are contained in the Weights and Measures Act. There are also a number of regulations on food labelling made by the EEC (for example compulsory date marking). Under these regulations the labels on all prepacked foods must display the following:

(a) the name of the food (or its variety or species), and any treatment it has received, such as smoking or freezing;

(b) a complete list of ingredients, including any preservatives, and the quantities added;

(c) a date mark, which should be based on the minimum durability of the food, during which time the food should retain its quality of freshness and suitability for consumption;

(d) instructions as to storage conditions for the product;

(e) the business name and address of the manufacturer or the seller of food within the EEC plus the country of origin should also appear;

(f) clear instructions as to how to prepare the food;

(g) if the manufacturer or seller of the food makes claims as to its qualities, such as being suitable for slimmers or diabetics, this must be explained on the label. In such circumstances, there must be directions as to how much food should be consumed and how often.

Equipment used for the weighing and measuring of food must be approved and officially stamped by an inspector appointed by the local authority. The equipment must be suitable for its specific purpose. All pre-packed food should display accurately on the label the quantity contained in the package or container.

In there is any complaint after the food has been sold, the seller or manufacturer of foods will have to show that he took reasonable precautions and exercised due diligence.

Under the Food Act of 1984, it is an offence for a person to allow food for sale which is in any way injurious to the consumer. The Act serves to protect purchasers with regard to the nature, substance and quality of food. There are regulations which control the composition of the food, the addition of substances during preparation, and the various treatments or processes to which the food is subjected during preparation.

Food must not be falsely described on the label, nor must it show a misleading picture or photograph of the contents on the package. It must be fit for human consumption and be prepared in sanitary and clean conditions. There are special provisions relating to the standards required for the production and treatment of milk.

The Food Act also makes provision for the analysis of food which is below standard. Many local authorities have their own sampling officer, and provide facilities for the examination of samples. The sampling officer is empowered to purchase samples of food which he thinks may fall below the required standard. He submits the sample to the public analyst for a detailed examination, although they may have to pay a fee for the service. Authorised council officers have powers of entry to business premises for the purpose of ascertaining that standards of hygiene and cleanliness are satisfactory.

Product liability

Manufacturers and others e.g. distributors, will soon have an additional liability for injuries caused by their products. The Consumer Protection Act 1987 implements in the UK the EEC Directive on product liability. The Directive is designed primarily to prevent the sort of tragedy caused by new drugs such as thalidomide. In such a case, unless the manufacturer can prove the special 'development risk' defence, he may be strictly liable and must compensate the injured party for the damage caused by the product.

5.14 Eating Out

All restaurants must display their prices, including VAT, so that they can be read before you sit down for the meal. If the VAT or service charges are not stated on the menu, you do not have to pay them. All you are obliged to pay is the amount stated on the menu. If a service charge is indicated, but the amount or percentage is not stated, you will have to pay a reasonable amount, provided of course that the service was satisfactory.

If you are dissatisfied with the food itself, you must complain to the manager of the establishment – obviously the more you have eaten the less substantial the complaint will be! If the meal has been prepared or served without reasonable skill and care you can refuse to pay the bill, or pay under protest and sue the restaurant for a return of the money.

Remember: It is best, if at all possible, to pay separately for pre-dinner drinks, to avoid the VAT and service charge being added to them in the total bill.

The restaurateur is entitled to refuse to serve you if you arrive drunk and disorderly, and may sue for lost profit if you fail to arrive when a table has been booked.

5.15 Advertising

The British Code of Advertising Practice lays down strict guidelines regarding the statements made in advertisements. All advertisements must be truthful, and not misleading. There are particularly strict rules governing the advertising of credit, alcohol and drugs. Complaints about advertising should be directed to the Advertising Standards Authority (see page 125 for the address).

Advertisements which are broadcast on the TV or radio come under extra scrutiny from the Independent Broadcasting Authority, which has issued a Code of Advertising Standards and Practice, containing an additional ban on the advertising of cigarettes, and certain other products. Complaints about TV or radio advertisements should be made to the Independent Broadcasting Authority's Advertising Control Department (see page 125 for the address).

5.16 Holidays

Many travel agents belong to the Association of British Travel Agents (ABTA) which was established in conjunction with the Office of Fair Trading, and which has drawn up a Code of Practice for its members. The Association encourages its members to follow the Code of Practice, and also offers some assistance to consumers should anything go wrong. Although it may be advisable to use an ABTA member, your legal rights will be the same whoever you choose.

Your legal rights are based on the contract which exists between you and the tour operator. The tour operator must provide you with the services stated in the brochure and on the booking form. These services must be of a reasonable standard and be described in an accurate way. If they are not, the tour operator is in breach of his contract and you will be able to sue for loss of enjoyment.

Booking

The following considerations should be taken into account when planning a holiday abroad:

(a) whether you will have to pay more for certain flights, such as weekend or day flights – very often, night flights are much cheaper;
(b) whether there are any additional charges, such as airport taxes or surcharges;
(c) whether transport has been arranged between the resort hotel and the airport;
(d) what sort of accommodation is being offered – is it half board, full board or bed and breakfast, and what facilities are offered with the accommodation;
(e) what the rate of exchange is, and whether this is likely to inflate the cost of your holiday dramatically:
(f) if you deal through an ABTA travel agent, he must inform you of the types of insurance available; you must find out whether this covers you adequately for medical expenses;
(g) you should read all the small print on holiday booking forms!

Ensure well before your depaarture date that your passport is valid and that you have all the necessary documentation and insurance for your destination.

Foreign laws

When travelling abroad you will be bound by the laws of the country you are visiting, and their system of justice may be far different from that in the UK.

If you are arrested, you may be released on bail, which may be very costly. Your tour operator may be able to help you. The British Consulate or High Commission should also be contacted, but you should be aware of the following:

- they cannot give you money except in very limited circumstances and then it will only be a loan;
- they cannot offer legal advice, or in any way interpret the local laws;
- they cannot pay bills on your behalf.

The Consulate will, however, be able to present your case to the local authorities on your behalf and liaise with the UK, but you will not receive preferable treatment just because you are foreign. In extreme cases, an extradition treaty may exist and you may be repatriated.

Customs

It is necessary to find out what customs regulations apply when visiting a foreign country. *Never* carry anything for anyone else, particularly a stranger, since you may be carrying illegal substances. When you return to the UK, you should declare everything you have bought from abroad (except of course all that is within the duty-free allowances). Customs officers have wide powers of search, but are expected to adhere to a Code of Practice.

5.17 Public Houses

Most people are affected by licensing laws in one form or another. Licences are needed for a variety of activities, one of the most common being for the sale and consumption of alcohol.

The Licensing Act 1964 lays down the regulations governing the opening hours of public houses. The Act defines the length of time for which the public house may be open to the public. The publican is not *obliged* to open his premises for the full length of time specified in the legislation, but he must be seen to be providing a reasonable service to the public. Failure to do so may result in the licensing authorities refusing to renew his licence.

Opening hours are extended for a 10 minute drinking up time (in Northern Ireland 30 minutes), during which alcohol purchased during the opening time may be consumed. Anything not finished that time must be left – it cannot be taken off the premises. Failure to abide by this rule can result in a heavy fine. However, where the alcohol has been served with a meal, the drinking up time may be extended to 30 minutes. As from 2nd May 1987, alcohol may be consumed in for example restaurants with meals between 3 pm and 5.30 pm, and on Sundays, Christmas Day and Good Friday between 2 pm and 7 pm.

There are a number of restrictions relating to children entering a bar – the part of the licensed premises mainly used for the sale or consumption of alcohol. Children under the age of 14 cannot go into a bar during opening hours; surprisingly, however, children over the age of five are permitted to consume alcohol on licensed premises, provided that they do not actually buy the alcohol themselves, and they do not consume it in the bar area.

Landlords have discretion to refuse entry or service to anyone they choose, provided that this action is not based upon racial or sexual discrimination.

In order to sell alcohol for consumption on the premises, a landlord must obtain an 'on-licence'. Any establishment which sells alcohol for consumption off the premises, will require an 'off-licence'. Such licences have to be granted by the local licensing authorities and renewed annually. The licence specifies the times during which alcohol may be sold. It is an offence to permit any alcohol bought from an off-licence to be consumed on the premises or immediately outside.

It is also possible for licensed premises to obtain extensions for particular occasions, so, for example, they may be allowed to stay open an hour or so longer on a particular night. An application has to be made to the local licensing magistrate in person, and the police have the right to raise an objection. If the magistrates refuse to grant a licence to the applicant, he will be able to appeal to the Crown Court.

5.18 Firearms

It is illegal to be in possession of a shotgun without previously obtaining a shotgun certificate from your local police, who have the discretion to refuse to grant the certificate if they feel that you are not a suitable person to possess a firearm. Failure to obtain the necessary certificate may render you liable to a maximum prison sentence of six months, and/or a £2,000 fine. It is also an offence for an individual to sell or give a shotgun to someone who does not possess a certificate and this could lead to a prison sentence or a fine or both.

If your application for a shotgun certificate is refused, you may appeal against the decision in the Crown Court; in Scotland the appeal should go to the sheriff court.

A shotgun certificate is not needed in the following circumstances:

(a) if you borrow a shotgun from the owner of private land for use solely on his land and in his presence;
(b) if you borrow a shotgun for use on artificial targets, and at a place and time approved by the relevant local police officer;
(c) if the gun is being used by a visitor from abroad who is in this country for a period of not more than 30 days in any 12 months.

Further offences under the Firearms Act are:

(a) to trade firearms and shotguns without being registered with the police as a firearms dealer;
(b) to shorten the barrel of a shotgun to less than 24 inches;
(c) to convert an imitation firearm into a lethal weapon;
(d) to be in possession of a firearm or ammunition with intent to injure anyone;
(e) to try and resist arrest by the use of a real or imitation firearm;
(f) to carry a real or imitation firearm with intent to commit a crime;
(g) to supply a firearm to anyone who is not legally permitted to be in possession of one.

An imitation firearm, that is one which has the appearance of a real firearm, needs a certificate, and if it can easily be converted into a real firearm, it cannot be purchased without a firearm certificate.

For age limits on the use of firearms, see page 84.

From 15th July 1987 it is an offence under the Crossbows Act to sell or hire a crossbow to a person under the age of 17.

5.19 Contact Points

National Consumer Council
20 Grosvenor Gardens
London SW1W 0DH
Tel: (01) 730 3469

A government aided independent body which lobbies local and national bodies on behalf of consumers.

Citizens' Advice Bureaux
(local addresses to be found in phone book)

Offers free advice on a wide range of legal matters, particularly consumer problems, and is a useful pre-solicitor step to finding out rights.

Consumers Association
14 Buckingham Street
London WC2N 6DS
Tel: (01) 839 1222

Publishes reports and statistics on consumer issues. Also offers a basic advisory service to consumers with legal problems.

Office of Fair Trading
Field House
Breams Buildings
London EC4A 1PR
Tel: (01) 242 2858

Performs a watchdog role on consumer legislation, advising the government on undesirable trade practices, devising Codes of Practice for trade associations. Offers help and advice to both consumers and traders alike, by publishing information in the form of leaflets and books.

Local Trading Standards Department
(addresses to be found in phone book)

Investigates complaints against traders, hotels and restaurateurs who have unfit descriptions etc.

Local Authority Environmental Health Departments
(addresses to be found in phone book)

Investigates complaints against traders, hotels and restaurateurs who have unfit premises or are selling unfit food.

Advertising Standards Authority
Brook House
Torrington Place
London WC1E 7HN
Tel: (01) 580 5555

Investigates advertisers who appear to have in some way breached the standards set by the Authority.

Independent Broadcasting Authority
70 Brompton Road
London SW3 1EY
Tel: (01) 584 7011

Investigates complaints about advertising on TV or Radio.

Trade associations

Will investigate complaints about members on behalf of consumers who have a grievance. Many have their own internal disciplinary procedures and may discipline members. Some also offer technical advice and assistance to customers.

Direct Selling Association
44 Russell Square
London WC1P 4JP
Tel: (01) 580 8433

'Direct selling' refers to goods sold at organised private parties and doorstep sales. Will investigate complaints against members and has disciplinary procedures.

Radio Electrical and Television Retailers Association
RETRA House
57–61 Newington Causeway
London SE1 6BE
Tel: (01) 403 1463

Trade association for retailers of the above products. Will investigate complaints against members and has disciplinary procedures.

The Mail Order Traders Association of Great Britain
25 Castle Street
Liverpool L2 4TD
Tel: (051) 236 7581

Trade association for mail order traders. Has code of practice and disciplinary powers over members, and offers help and advice to consumers who have complaints against such traders.

Mail Order Protection Scheme
16 Tooks Court
London EC4A 1LB
Tel: (01) 405 6806

A scheme run by national newspapers to protect consumers against advertisers who go into liquidation.

Association of British Laundry Cleaning and Rental Services
Lancaster Gate House
319 Pinner Road
Harrow
Middlesex HA1 4HX
Tel: (01) 863 7755

Trade association which also issues a code of practice for members and has disciplinary powers which may be enforced against those members who fall below the prescribed standards.

Banking Ombudsman
Citadel House
5/11 Fetter Lane
London EC4A 1BR
Tel: (01) 583 1395

Investigates complaints by individual customers and groups of individuals such as partnerships or clubs against banks. The scheme is not available to companies.

Electricity Consumers Council
Brook House
Torrington Place
London WC1E 7LL
Tel: (01) 636 5703

Will put consumers in touch with local regional council, the address of which can also be found on the back of the electricity bill.

Gas Consumer Council
4th Floor
162/168 Regent Street
London W1R 5TB
Tel: (01) 439 0012

An independent body set up by Parliament to assist consumers on a variety of matters such as gas prices, gas supply, the availability of spare parts and service efficiency.

OFGAS
2nd Floor
South Side
105 Victoria Street
London SW1E 6QT
Tel: (01) 828 0898

Independent regulatory authority monitoring British Gas operations in the interest of tariff customers.

British Telecom Users Association
34 Grand Avenue
London N10 3BP
Tel: (01) 883 7229

Investigates complaints against BT by consumers with regard to charging, service, efficiency etc.

OFTEL
Atlantic House
Holborn Viaduct
London EC1N 2HQ

Tel: (01) 353 4020

An independent body set up by the DTI as a regulatory authority, monitoring British Telecom operations on behalf of customers.

Post Office Users National Council
Waterloo Bridge House
Waterloo Road
London SE1 8UA
Tel: (01) 928 49458

Investigates complaints against the Post Office concerning charging, service, efficiency etc.

Central Transport Consultative Committee
1st Floor, Golden Cross House
Duncannon Street
London WC2N 4JF
Tel: (01) 839 7338/9

A consumer organisation which looks after British Rail travellers and consults with BR about performance.

Association of British Travel Agents (ABTA)
55–57 Newman Street
London W1P 4AH
Tel: (01) 637 2444

Chartered Institute of Arbitrators
75 Cannon Street
London EC4N 5BH
Tel: (01) 236 8761

Will supply professional arbitration service to try and settle a variety of disputes before they reach court.

6. Employment Matters

Employment is another area which has seen the development of a mass of new provisions over past years – all aimed at improving the lot of the employee. This chapter provides a brief overview of the most important elements.

6.1 Contract of Employment

Everyone who is employed by another is under a contract of employment. This may be written or oral, but by law the employer must provide the employee with certain minimum written particulars within 13 weeks of the commencement of the employment.

Although the written particulars do not necessarily form the actual contract, they are valuable evidence of it. Only employees, *not* independent contractors or the self employed, have the protection of the employment legislation. The distinction is really whether the contract is one *of* service, or one *for* services; the former characterises an employee, the latter is usually indicative of an independent contractor.

The minimum written particulars of a contract of employment must include the following:

- the names of the employer and the employee;
- the date of commencement of the employment;
- the salary at commencement, and how often it is paid;
- normal working hours;
- holiday entitlement;
- company rules concerning absence/sickness;
- pension arrangements;
- period of notice required on either side;
- the employee's job title;
- the disciplinary rules and procedures.

A code of practice set up under the old Industrial Relations Act states that the following are also recommended for inclusion in the written particulars:

- the specific requirements of the job and the direct line of authority for the employee;
- trade union arrangements;
- promotion and training opportunities;
- social and welfare facilities;
- health and safety rules and procedures.

Employment contracts are broadly similar to other contracts with regard to the offer and acceptance of employment, the enforceabilty of terms, its termination and the effect of breaches. The terms of the contract can be extended by custom and practice at the work place. A very serious act of misconduct by the employee can instantly terminate the contract without the need for notice. Similarly certain acts by the employer can terminate the contract and demonstrate to the employee that the contract of employment has been brought to an end.

Implied terms

Implied terms of employment contracts are those which are not spelled out in the actual contract of employment but which the courts have considered should form an integral part of every contract of employment.

Thus employers must:

- provide a wage for employees;
- provide a safe work place, by ensuring that all equipment used by the employee is safe, that all other staff are competent; that adequate supervision and instruction are provided.

Although the employer is under a duty to pay his staff, he is not under a duty to provide work unless he has agreed to do so, as, for example, in the case of an apprentice.

Employees must:

- observe working hours, and produce work up to a reasonable standard;
- obey all lawful and reasonable orders from their boss, and take reasonable care in carrying out the orders;
- observe confidentiality;
- always act in the best interests of the employer.

Wages

If you work full time you should receive an itemised statement of your pay, setting out clearly all deductions and the reasons for them, and indicating the basis on which the figures hav been calculated. If the employer fails to provide such a statement, you are entitled to ask an industrial tribunal to order the employer to provide this information.

If the employer overpays you, you must expect to pay that money back, since you are not allowed to keep money which has been paid to you in error.

Sickness

Your entitlement or otherwise to sick pay will be determined either by the contract of employment itself or by the written particulars. Generally speaking, you are entitled to statutory sick pay ('SSP') during your first eight weeks off work through illness, provided that:

(a) you are sick for at least four consecutive days (including Sundays and Public Holidays); and
(b) you notify your employer of your absence; and
(c) you submit evidence of your illness, for example a doctor's certificate, to your employer.

The payment need not be made for the first three 'qualifying' days of the period of absence. A qualifying day is any day on which the employee would normally be required to work.

If you are not fit enough to return to work after eight weeks, SSP finishes. You must apply to the DHSS for State sickness benefit and enquire whether you are entitled to any other state benefits. If your employer does not pay SSP, you must claim sickness benefits from the DHSS.

Hours of work

You must work the number of hours specified in your contract or written particulars. In certain cases the contract may specifically require you to work overtime, if requested to do so, with or without extra pay; if there is no such clause in the contract then in theory you may refuse to do so.

Termination of the contract of employment

The law has laid down minimum periods of notice which apply unless the contract or the written particulars provide for longer periods. Unless the termination is the result of an act of gross misconduct, when instant dismissal is allowed, both parties must give the statutory minimum period of notice. The period of notice required is determined by the length of service and may, by agreement, be extended in the written contract of employment. Employees with over one month's service must give a minimum of one week's notice. The statutory minimum periods of notice required to be given by employers is as follows:

Length of employment	Statutory minimum notice by employer
Less than 1 month	none
1 month – 2 years	1 week
2 – 12 years	1 week for each full year of employment
12 years and more	12 weeks

If you are a senior employee a court might feel that a longer notice period is reasonable – for example a managing director might reasonably expect 6–12 months' notice depending on length of service.

The employer does not necessarily have to keep you in work once he has given you notice – he may give you wages in lieu of notice, the amount of the payment being determined by the amount of notice. However, he must give you the proper period of notice, even if there is no work.

On being dismissed after at least six months of employment, you are entitled to a written explanation of the reasons for the dismissal, but you must ask the employer for this. The written reasons must be supplied within 14 days of your application. If your employer fails to comply with the request, an industrial tribunal may make an award to you of two weeks pay.

References

An employer is under no legal obligation to provide a reference. If he does so, he must tell the truth, and must not be malicious.

6.2 Maternity Rights

If you become pregnant you are entitled to a number of maternity rights, provided that you have been continuously employed (full time) for a minimum period of two years, by the same employer, although there is no qualifying period for entitlement to time off with pay in order to attend ante-natal clinics.

You are also entitled to maternity pay, provided that in addition to the two years continuous employment requirement, you comply with the following:

(a) you must stay at work until at least the 11th week before the expected date of birth;

(b) before you leave you must tell your employer that you intend to stop work because of your pregnancy; it is always advisable to give this notice in writing, although it is not absolutely necessary.

If you have left your job because of pregnancy, you have the right to return to work, provided that:

(a) you were employed until the 11th week before the expected date of birth;

(b) you had been employed for a minimum period of two years at the beginning of the 11th week before confinement;

(c) you have given notice to your employer, at least 2 days before your absence began, or your intention to give up work because of the pregnancy, and that you would want to return to work.

You will also have to give written confirmation of your intention to return to work seven weeks after the expected date of birth (even if this is not the actual date of birth), if requested to do so by your employer. Your right to return will cease if you do not confirm your intention within 14 days.

You must return to work within 29 weeks of the birth, and give your employer three weeks written warning of your intention to do so.

In some cases the employer will take a replacement for the time during which you are off for the birth. It is perfectly fair for the employer to dismiss the replacement when you return to work, provided that the replacement was aware of the short term nature of the employment.

You may return to do the same work as before, or you may be offered a suitable alternative, which should not be unreasonably refused.

6.3 Disciplinary Rules and Procedures

The following should be observed by an employer when faced with having to discipline an employee. He should:

(a) inform you that a complaint has been made against you, and the nature of that complaint;

(b) give you a chance to put your side of the story;

(c) apply the appropriate disciplinary action, which will normally be one of the following measures, depending on the seriousness of the matter:

- an informal oral warning;
- a formal written warning;
- a further written warning where another breach has occurred.

6.4 Unfair Dismissal

Every employee has the right not to be unfairly dismissed by his or her employer, and if covered by the unfair dismissal legislation, to complain to an industrial tribunal. Whenever a complaint of unfair dismissal is made to an industrial tribunal, the services of a conciliation officer are available to either party to help reach a settlement.

If you take your complaint to an industrial tribunal, it is for you to show that you were dismissed, and for the employer to show that the reason for the dismissal was fair.

A *dismissal* is defined as occurring only if:

(a) your contract of employment is terminated by your employer with or without notice; *or*

(b) you work under a fixed term contract and the term of it expires without renewal under the same contract; *or*

(c) you terminate your own contract with or without notice in circumstances such that you are entitled to do so because of your employer's conduct towards you. This is called constructive dismissal. An example of constructive dismissal is where the employer makes major adverse changes in the terms of the employment contract without prior consultation. In effect, the employer has made it impossible for you to continue working for him.

A person may be *fairly* dimissed on one of the following grounds:

- misconduct
- incapability
- redundancy
- some other substantial reason
- that continued employment would breach a statutory duty.

An important factor which the tribunal considers is the disciplinary steps which preceded the dismissal. They must be fair and reasonable and must be applied in every disciplinary case. In any event, the way the dismissal is handled should not breach the unwritten rules of natural justice, for example that you should be given the right of reply and be consulted throughout.

To qualify for protection against unfair dismissal you must generally have been in continuous employment with the same employer for two years.

Industrial tribunals

Many industrial relations disputes are decided by industrial tribunals. The tribunal is administered by a clerk and consists of three people – a chairman who is legally qualified, and two lay members nominated from either side of industry. The aim of the tribunal is to provide a less formal means of settling industrial disputes than that offered by the courts, and either side may represent themselves or be represented by anyone else, not necessarily a lawyer. Sometimes a case is dealt with under a vetting procedure known as a 'pre-hearing assessment', where a decision is taken as to whether the case warrants a full hearing and, if not, whether the proceeding party will risk a costs award against them if they lose.

Very strict time limits are imposed on referring cases to tribunals – an action for unfair dismissal must be brought within three months of the effective date of termination of employment, even if the employee concerned has spent time going through internal appeals procedures to try and get his job back. Professional advice should be sought when considering taking action for unfair dismissal.

Appeals from decisions made by industrial tribunals go to the Employment Appeals Tribunal, except in Northern Ireland where they go to the Court of Appeal.

Remedies for unfair dismissal

If the tribunal finds that the dismissal was unfair, it may order that you be given your old job back on the same terms as before, or that you should be taken back by your employer, but offered a reasonable alternative job. This rarely happens in practice and the most common remedy is compensation, which may comprise three elements which can be reduced by your own 'contributory fault'.

(a) *basic award* – this is a statutory figure which is related to your length of service;

(b) *compensatory award* – which reflects the loss you have suffered because of your employer's action, any expenses you have incurred and benefits lost as a result of the dismissal;

(c) *an additional award* – for your employer's failure to comply with a reengagement or reinstatement order.

6.5 Redundancy

Redundancy is the dismissal of an employee as a direct result of there being no work for him/her to do, for example where the firm closes down or when key contracts are lost. If you are made redundant you will be entitled to a redundancy payment from your employer, subject to the minimum amount specified in the employment legislation.

In order to qualify for redundancy payments however, you must satisfy the following conditions:

- you must have worked for your employer for at least two years;
- you must have been dismissed;
- you must be redundant as defined by law.

The employer may avoid his liability to make a redundancy payment if he can offer another job. You will also lose your entitlement if you refuse this job unreasonably and your employer can show that the alternative job was suitable.

6.6 Wrongful Dismissal

Wrongful dismissal is the dismissal of an employee in contravention of his contract of employment, for example by not giving the proper notice period or payment in lieu. Instant dismissal without notice is permissible *only* in cases where the employee has committed an act of gross misconduct or incompetence. If such a dismissal is unjustified, and the employee falls outside the unfair dismissal legislation, he may bring a claim against the employer in the ordinary courts for breach of contract based on the wrongful dismissal.

Proceedings are in court, not in an industrial tribunal. The cost of pursuing a wrongful dismissal action may be high and the award of damages, if successful, may be low. A wrongful dismissal claim does not allow the employee to apply for reinstatement. The court limits its assessment of damages to the amount which the employee would have received if they had not been wrongfully dismissed.

6.7 Equal Pay

The equal pay legislation aims to ensure that employees are not discriminated against on grounds of sex, in terms of payment for their work. The employees must be doing the same or similar work, at the same place and for the same employer before they can bring an action under the legislation.

If a woman's job has been rated as equivalent to a man's job under a job evaluation scheme, the woman will be entitled to the same rate of pay, trms and conditions of employment as the man. Remember, the work does not have to be *exactly* the same. It must be broadly similar. The issue will normally be decided by an industrial tribunal.

If you decide that you wish to bring an equal pay claim, you should seek specialist advice from a trade union, a solicitor or some other professional advisor.

6.8 Trade Unions

Generally speaking, employees have the right to join a trade union and any attempt by an employer to stop such membership is illegal. Trade union related dismissals attract higher compensation awards known as 'special awards'. Any form of victimisation or discrimination for trade union activities on the part of the employer is illegal if the activities are carried on outside working hours (excluding official meal times etc).

If the employer recognises a trade union, then he must be prepared to allow trade union representatives and officials some time off for carrying out official duties.

Closed shops (ie where all employees are obliged, except in certain circumstances, to join a specific union) are prominent in many industries. Before it can be considered lawful, the closed shop has to be voted in by the employees in a secret ballot, and approved by an 80 per cent majority. If the closed shop is voted in, the employer has to insist upon employees within the firm joining the union in question. When a closed shop comes into force, any existing employees who not wish wish to join cannot be compelled to do so. Every closed shop must ballot its members every five years in order to remain lawful—again an 80 per cent majority is required.

There are a number of circumstances in which the employee may lawfully refuse to join the closed shop. For example, an employee may have a conscientious or deeply held personal objection to joining the union; this may apply to a particular union or to unions in general. In such cases, a dismissal by the employer for refusing to join will be regarded as unfair, giving the employee the right to take the employer to a tribunal.

Trade unions must be seen to act reasonably in their dealings with their members. If anyone is expelled from the union he may take his case to an industrial tribunal, which will examine the circumstances of the case. If it finds the union to be at fault, the tribunal can order the union to reinstate the employee and pay compensation. This order must be complied with within four weeks otherwise the compensation order may be increased.

6.9 The Advisory Conciliation and Arbitration Service—ACAS

This is a body which operates independently of the government, and is designed to promote the improvement of industrial relations and the extension of collective bargaining. ACAS may hold its own inquiries if it so wishes, but usually operates to resolve industrial disputes where the parties involved consistently fail to reach any form of agreement. It supervises the work of conciliation officers who can be used to assist in the settlement of disputes which would otherwise go to an industrial tribunal hearing.

Either party in an industrial dispute is entitled to consult ACAS, and although there is no obligation for both sides to co-operate, it is generally in their interests to do so. It acts through Conciliation Officers.

ACAS has drawn up voluntary codes of practice, which lay down the recommended rules and procedures with regard to matters such as discipline, union activities and picketing.

6.10 Wages Councils

Wages councils offer protection to employees (over the age of 21) in industries where in general no trade union exists, and set statutory minimum rates of pay, holiday entitlement, and other terms of the contract. The industries having wages councils include retailing, catering and textile manufacturing. The council will set the minimum rates of pay by means of wages orders which the relevant employers are legally bound to observe. Employees who are under-paid can ask the local inspector to investigate the case on their behalf.

6.11 Industrial Safety

There is a great deal of legislation concerning the health, safety and welfare of employees. The Health and Safety at Work Act 1974 places a duty on employers to provide clean and safe work places. In particular it requires employers to ensure that:

Health

(a) the workplace is kept clean and hygienic;
(b) the workplace is not overcrowded;
(c) a reasonable temperature is maintained;
(d) there is adequate ventilation throughout the premises;
(e) there is adequate lighting;

Safety

(f) all dangerous machinery, and all dangerous parts of machinery, are adequately guarded. The machinery will be regarded as dangerous if danger may reasonably be anticipated from its use without protection;
(g) dangerous machinery is positioned and constructed safely, and regularly maintained;

(h) dangerous substances are secured – all reasonable precautions must be taken to ensure the safety of all employees who come or who may come into contact with the substance;

(i) floors, stairs and passages are of sound construction and properly maintained; they must be kept free from obstruction or slippery substances;

Welfare

(j) adequate supplies of drinking water are available;

(k) there are suitable washing facilities;

(l) suitable first aid facilities and someone trained to administer first aid when necessary are provided.

The employer owes a duty of care to every person working or employed on the premises.

6.12 Contact Points

Equal Opportunities Commission

Overseas House	St Andrew House	Chamber of Commerce House
Quay Street	141 West Nile Street	22 Great Victoria Street
Manchester M3 3HN	Glasgow G1 2RN	Belfast BT2 7BA
Tel. (061) 833 9244	Tel. (041) 332 8018	Tel. (0232) 242752

Established in 1975 to ensure effective enforcement of the Sex Discrimination Act and the Equal Pay Act. Responsible for eliminating discrimination in employment, education and training opportunities and in the provision of goods, facilities and services. Also investigates areas of inequality and makes recommendations to the Government about existing law and possible improvements.

Commission for Racial Equality
Elliot House   Scotland: 031 226 5189
10/12 Allington Street   031 225 4323.
London SW1E 5EH
Tel. (01) 828 7022

Works towards the elimination of discrimination, the promotion of equality of opportunity and good relations between different racial groups. It makes recommendations for changes when necessary. Can conduct formal investigations and is empowered to require production of information to assist the investigation.

Equal Pay and Opportunity Campaign
45 College Cross
London N1 1PT

Pressure group campaigning for women's rights in employment and the trade unions.

Industrial Tribunals
Central Office of Industrial Tribunals

93 Ebury Bridge Road	St Andrews House	Bedford House
London SW1W 8RE	141 West Nile Street	16–22 Bedford Street
Tel. (01) 730 9161	Glasgow G1 2RU	Belfast BT2 7NR
	Tel. (041) 331 1601	Tel. (0232) 227 666

Industrial tribunals are independent judicial bodies with permanent offices in larger towns. The central office deals with the administration of tribunals in London and is the HQ of the regional offices of which there are sixteen in England and Wales.

ACAS
Head Office
11–12 St James's Square
London SW1Y 7RA
Tel. (01) 210 3655

123/125 Bothwell Street
Glasgow G2 7JR
Tel. (041) 204 2677

Set up in 1974 and given statutory powers in 1975. Offers impartial advice to management, unions and employees with the purpose of improving industrial relations.

Office of the Wages Council

11 Tothill Street	Pentland House	13 Bloomfield Avenue
London SW1H 9NF	Robb's Loan	Belfast BT5 5HD
Tel. (01) 213 3881	Edinburgh EH14 1UE	Tel. (0232) 226201
	Tel. (031) 443 8731	

Empowered under the Wages Act 1986 to make orders fixing basic rates of pay, overtime rates, and amounts deductible for living accommodation.

Health and Safety Executive

Baynards House	St Hugh's House	Broad Lane
1 Chepstow Place	Trinity Road	Sheffield
London W2 4TF	Bootle L20 3QY	S3 7HQ
Tel. (01) 229 3456	Tel. (051) 951 4381	Tel. (0742) 75239

Scotland East–   Scotland West–
Belford House   314 St Vincent Street
Belford Road   Glasgow G3 8XG
Edinburgh EH4 3UE   Tel. (041) 204 2646
Tel. (031) 225 1313

Northern Ireland Department of Economic Development
Health and Safety Legislation Branch
83 Lades Drive
Belfast BT6 9FJ
Tel: (0232) 701444 Ext 283

A statutory body appointed by the Health and Safety Commission which
will work in accordance with directions and guidance given by the Commission.
Will also enforce legal requirements and provide an advistory service to both
sides of industry.

7. Accidents

Although there is no legal definition of the term accident, an accident is generally taken to mean any unexpected or unintended event which causes loss or damage to another. If it is an event for which no-one is to blame, possibly an 'Act of God', then, apart from insurance (discussed in the next chapter), there is no legal remedy. Except in cases of strict liability (see below), damages can only be claimed if fault can be proved, and if it can be shown that someone has been negligent.

7.1 Negligence

Generally speaking a duty of care is owed to those around us, and we should not act in a manner likely to cause them personal injury or damage to their property.

If you are injured by anyone, the law states that there are three fundamental points which must be proved before their liability to you can be established, giving you the right to sue them for damages:

(a) you must be owed a duty of care;
(b) that duty of care must have been breached; and
(c) that breach of duty must have caused your injury.

As a motorist for example, you have a duty of care to passengers in your car and to pedestrians and other motorists, and you must not drive in a way which may cause them harm.

If you wish to bring an action against the person who injured you, you will also have to show that the defendant (in Scotland, 'defender') foresaw that his actions could lead to injury – the law is somewhat unclear on the extent to which this 'foreseeability' test applies, and every case must be decided upon its facts. The test applied by the courts in such cases is whether, in the normal course of events, a person of reasonable intelligence would have been able to foresee the harm. So that if you are acting in a dangerous manner and you injure someone, you are more likely to be liable to the person you have injured than if you were acting normally and not doing anything which might be considered dangerous by most people.

If you have been trained in a particular profession, and have consequently acquired a specialised skill, you will owe a greater duty of care to those who rely on your skill. If you are a doctor for example, you will owe a duty of care to your patients, and failure on your part to exercise that skill properly, will leave you liable in negligence should damage or injury be caused by your actions. The harm caused must have been a direct result of your failure to exercise a level of skill commensurate with your position and qualifications.

Sometimes the duty of care extends even to those circumstances in which it is impossible to foresee that the harm could occur. For example, if you jump out on someone who has a weak heart and they suffer a heart attack, you will be liable for the injury. The saying is 'you take your victim as you find him'.

Claiming damages

The purpose of awarding damages in a civil case is not to penalise the person who has caused the injury, but to compensate the victim for the loss he has suffered as a result of the injury or damage. The loss suffered is quantifiable, the amount depending on the circumstances of the case. It is possible for an experienced litigation lawyer to estimate the amount of damages appropriate to a particular case by referring to previous similar cases.

Damages are made up of several elements, which are known as 'heads of damage'. These are:

(a) special damages, for the financial loss suffered up to the date of the court hearing; and
(b) general damages, which include damages for:
- the injury itself;
- pain and suffering (including mental anguish);
- loss of amenity or enjoyment of life;
- other matters including disfigurement, depression and nervous shock;
- medical care, including private treatment.

Deductions will be made from the final award if you have received certain State benefits. You are expected to 'mitigate' your loss if at all possible. For example, if you have lost your job as a result of the accident, you should try to find suitable alternative employment.

Personal injury claims very often take several years to be heard in the courts, partly because the legal system is slow and partly because it is necessary to wait some time for the full extent of the injuries suffered to become fully apparent.

It is not absolutely necessary to prove physical damage in order to claim compensation for negligence. Anyone who suffers nervous shock as a result of someone else's breach of duty of care may have a claim against that person. For example a person who sees an accident and believes that her children have been involved, and consequently suffers nervous shock, may sue the negligent person.

Contributory negligence

If the injured person is in any way to blame for the harm which has come to him, any damages he may receive will be proportionately reduced, even if the person at fault is grossly negligent. Examples are not wearing seat belts or crash helmets. Any attempt to exclude liability for personal injury or death caused by negligence by means of exclusion clauses in a contract will be ineffective at law (see page 37).

Time limits

Negligence claims must be commenced within six years of the date of occurrence. However, the Latent Damage Act provides special time limits for certain negligence claims which have no element of personal injury.

Personal injury cases must be commenced within three years from the date of the accident, or from the date on which the victim first realised that he had been injured and that he could sue for damages. Proceedings must have been instituted within that time limit — it does not matter that the case does not reach the courts in that time.

'Strict liability'

This term was first introduced into English law by the case of *Rylands* v *Fletcher*. In that case, it was decided that any person who keeps anything on his land or property which is likely to cause damage if it escapes, does so at his own risk, and will be liable for all damage which occurs as a direct result of that escape.

The decision in that case is now applied to all circumstances in which a person keeps anything which is potentially dangerous, such as wild animals, or dangerous substances. If any damage is caused by its escape, the owner will be strictly liable, no matter how many precautions he took to prevent the escape. In such cases, negligence does not have to be proved in order for a claim to be successful.

7.2 Accidents

Road accidents

The Road Traffic Act states that anyone involved in a road accident must stop and give their name and address to anyone else concerned if:

- anyone has been injured;
- any other vehicle has been damaged;
- any animal listed in the Road Traffic Acts (which does not include a cat) has been injured; or
- any damage has been caused to property.

If no one else is involved, for example if a car has a collision with a wall, the driver must take steps to report the accident to the police as soon as reasonably practicable, which must be within 24 hours. If the motorist can prove that he did not know that he had been part of the accident then he cannot be charged with an offence. However, this will obviously be a difficult matter to prove.

At the scene of an accident it is useful to note the following:

- registration number(s) of the vehicles involved;
- name(s) and address(es) of the other people involved;
- postion(s) of the vehicles at the time of the accident;
- time of the accident and general weather conditions at that time;
- name(s) and address(es) of any witnesses;
- amount of damage done to the vehicles involved.

If anyone is injured insurance details must be exchanged.

The police should be called if an offence has been committed, if anyone is injured or if the other drivers refuse to give the necessary details.

In Scotland, any accidents should, as a general rule, be reported to the police as soon as reasonably practicable.

Do not:

- behave aggressively towards other driver(s) – this will make matters worse for you;
- admit responsibility for the accident;
- move the vehicles until a note of their positions has been made.

Accidents at work

As was stated in the chapter on employment, every employer has the duty, as far as reasonably practicable, to ensure that the employee's working conditions and environment are reasonably safe. Failure to do so may render him liable in negligence, with, in addition, financial penalties under the Health and Safety regulations. The employer must take reasonable care for the welfare of his staff in the following areas:

- to ensure that all staff are competent, and do not represent a danger to others;
- to ensure that equipment and plant are of a safe standard;
- to provide a safe system of working for employees.

If you are injured at work:

(a) if there are any witnesses to the accident, make a note of their name(s); you may need to obtain a written statement from them;
(b) inform the employer of the accident and ensure that a record is made in the accident book;
(c) keep any evidence of the accident;
(d) if you are a trade union member contact your representative;
(e) consider taking legal advice.

An employer must inform the local authority of any accident which causes serious injury or death, and any major incidents which represent a danger or hazard, whether or not injury has in fact resulted. The employer must also report to the Health and Safety Executive any accident which results in any employee being off work for more than three days.

Employers have to take out insurance policies to protect themselves against claims for industrial injury, and provide compensation for an injured employee. The amount of the compensation will be assessed by the court, and will be dependent upon the seriousness of the injury and the loss of earnings which are a direct result of the accident. Damages are also paid for any future loss, for example, if after the accident the employee is incapable of performing the same type of work, and loss of amenity and enjoyment of life.

The employer must provide a system of work which will enable employees to carry out their duties without being subject to unnecessary risk. If, for example, you are injured by lifting something at work, the following points must be considered to decide whether or not a claim against your employer:

(a) whether or not you received any training in lifting techniques;
(b) whether there was any assistance available either from other employees, or from lifting machinery;
(c) whether or not you followed the usual method of lifting that particular object and the possibility that you may have been partly to blame.

If you are injured by defective equipment, your employer will be strictly liable even if the injury was caused by negligence on the part of the manufacturer of the defective equipment.

The employer is under a legal duty to keep floors free of substances likely to cause people to slip; there should be some sort of system whereby if anything does get spilt on the floor, it is removed as soon as possible. If there is such a system which is reasonably efficient, then there is very little chance of there being a successful personal injury claim against the employer, since he has taken all reasonable precautions to ensure the safety of his employees.

A number of accidents are also caused by over polished floors, rather than spillages, and employers should ensure that non-slip polish is used in order to protect his employees from injury.

If accidents occur during icy conditions on the employer's premises, and reasonable steps have been taken to reduce the risk, the employer will not in general be liable for any personal injury suffered.

Accidents at school

During the time pupils are in the care of a school, the teachers are under a duty to take reasonable care of the children (they are *'in loco parentis'*). If any accident occurs which results in injury to a child, and it can be shown that the school teachers failed in their duty, then the school will be liable in negligence. If the school is private the action will lie against the governing body of the school; if it is a state school, it will lie against the local authority. The child will be able to take legal action for damages for the injuries received, an the parents will also be able to sue for expenses incurred as a result of the child's injury, such as travel or accommodation expenses.

Accidents at home

As was explained on page 61, if any person is injured on your premises as a result of your negligence, you will be liable for the damage or injury. So for example, if you knew of the existence of a danger, such as loose roof tiles, and failed to do anything about it, you will be liable to the person who suffered injury. This rule only applies to invited people, and does not extend to squatters or burglars.

There are a number of legal requirements with regard to safety in the home which relate specifically to children. Under the Children and Young Persons Act, it is an offence for any person who is responsible for a child under the age of 12 to leave the child alone in a room with a heater or fire without a fireguard.

Under the health and safety legislation, local authorities are obliged to ensure their their recreation areas for children are safe. Inspectors ensure that regular maintenance checks are carried out. Any member of the public who is aware of a danger is entitled to report it to the local authority, who will make an investigation.

If a child is injured in a public playground it will only be possible to sue if it can be proved that the local authority responsible for the playground has been negligent.

In certain circumstances, no matter how many precautions have been taken, the owners of premises which are regarded by the law as an 'allurement' will carry a risk of liability. A common example is railway lines, which are a constant attraction to children. British Rail is potentially liable for any injury suffered, no matter how careful they have been to fence off the danger.

Sporting accidents

As a general rule, sporting competitors and spectators consent to the risk of injury which may come about during the normal course of the sport concerned. Boxers, for example, consent to the damage caused by a blow to the head, provided that it is delivered during the lawful course of the fight. Any injury which is sustained outside the rules of the sport in question will give the victim the right to sue for damages, or prosecute for assault as has been seen in Rugby Union.

7.3 Criminal Injuries

If you have received injury as a result of a crime of violence, you may apply to the Criminal Injuries Compensation Board for compensation. In order to be eligible, the police must have been informed, and the injuries received must be severe enough to warrant a compensatory award of at least £550. You will not be eligible if you have been injured as a result of a traffic offence, unless someone deliberately tried to run you over.

The Board will have regard to the severity of the injuries, and the financial loss you have suffered, when considering the amount of compensation.

There is no Criminal Injuries Compensation Board in Northern Ireland; cases are determined on the basis of medical evidence by the Northern Ireland Office and appeals may be made to the county court. The amount claimed must be at least £250, or £1,000 for nervous shock.

7.4 Contact Points

Action for the Victims of Medical Accidents
24 Southwark Street
London SE1 1TY
Tel. (01) 403 4744

An advisory service for victims of medical negligence. Holds a list of specialist lawyers and medical experts.

The Patients Association
Room 33
18 Charing Cross Road
London WC2H OHR
Tel. (01) 240 0671

An advice service which aims to present and further the interests of patients.

Medical Victims Association
137 Morriston Road
Elgin Scotland IV30 2NB
Tel. (0343) 41339

Criminal Injuries Compensation Board
19–30 Alfred Place
London WC1E 7EG
Tel. (01) 636 9501

Makes awards of financial compensation to victims of crimes of violence where the severity of the injury caused warrants a claim of £550 or more.

Fire Protection Association
140 Aldersgate Street
London EC1A 4HX
Tel. (01) 606 3757

Provides advice on all aspects of the causes and prevention of fire.

Royal Society for the Prevention of Accidents
Cannon House
The Priory
Queensway
Birmingham B4 6BS
Tel. (021) 200 2461

8. Insurance

8.1 The Policy

An insurance policy covers you against loss resulting from the occurrence of certain specified events. If you insure your home against damage from fire or flooding for example, the insurance company will compensate you for the loss, provided that you have paid your premium and no exceptions apply to your case.

The insurance policy is a contract between you (the proposer) and the insurer, which can be a company authorised to transact insurance, or an underwriter or a syndicate of underwriters at Lloyds of London. The 'consideration' for that contract is your payment of the premium. The insurer's obligation is then to meet your claim if it arises out of a risk covered by the policy. The contract is said to be founded 'on utmost good faith'.

When taking out insurance you will be asked to complete a proposal form which requests certain information and requires you to state any additional information which might affect the risk proposed. The contents of the proposal will determine the rate of premium, the acceptance of the risk and the need for any special conditions, and forms a vital part of the contract. If you fail to tell the insurer of all material facts, whether requested or not, then in the event of a claim the insurer will have the right to reject the claim. This is termed 'non-disclosure of a material fact', and the duty to disclose applies every time you renew a policy other than a life assurance or a permanent health policy.

On receipt of your policy, read it carefully and ensure that it covers the risks and amounts you require and that all other details are correct. The policy will have conditions and exclusions and this 'small print' needs to be read carefully and understood.

When you are considering taking out a policy there are two principal routes open to you; you may insure either through an insurance broker or directly with the insurance company.

8.2 Brokers

The broker usually acts as the agent of the proposer, and in most cases provides his advice free of charge since he earns his income from commision from insurers whose policies he sells. It is advisable to check that the broker you are dealing with has expertise in the type of cover you seek and will find you the best cover for the most competitive premium.

For an individual or company to term itself an insurance broker, they must comply with the Insurance Brokers (Registration) Act 1977 and any failure on their part could result in disciplinary action by the Insurance Brokers Registration Council. A broker must also take out professional indemnity insurance to ensure he can meet any compensation awarded if he is sued by customers to whom he gave negligent advice.

8.3 Insurance Companies

Major insurance companies have offices in most towns, and some operate direct sales forces with representatives who will call by oppointment to discuss your needs. Always bear in mind when dealing directly with an insurer that they will only promote their own policies, and therefore it is recommended that you approach several companies for quotations.

8.4 Claims

If you wish to claim under an insurance policy you should contact the insurance broker or insurance company as soon as possible. In most cases it will be necessary for you to complete a claim form, and on receipt of the form the insurance company will decide what action to take. If the claim is under a motor insurance policy they may instruct a motor engineer to inspect your vehicle, or if under a home policy, a loss adjuster to make an independent assessment of the damage.

If you feel that the insurance company has not dealt with your claim fairly then you can raise the matter with the Association of British Insurers or the Insurance Ombudsman if your insurance company subscribes to this scheme. A further alternative for insurance claims grievances is the Personal Insurance Arbitration Service.

8.5 Types of Insurance

As a private individual your insurance needs will generally be divided between cover for the person, and cover for your property or possessions. The main types of policy available are noted below.

Personal accident and sickness insurance

This type of policy provides fixed benefits, either in the form of a lump sum or a weekly payment, following an accident causing personal injury or death, or incapacity during sickness. The proposal form will ask questions concerning your health and any dangerous hobbies you may have, such a hang-gliding or rock-climbing. The insurance company may be prepared to cover such risks for an additional premium. You may be requested to undergo a medical examination in certain circumstances.

Under such a policy, you are required to confirm your health and personal circumstances at each renewal.

Remember: If you are injured as a result of someone else's negligence you may be able to sue them for damages/compensation in addition to claiming the above benefits.

Permanent health insurance

This cover is occasionally provided by employers as a 'fringe benefit' for their employees. A policy normally provides a set percentage – usually 75 per cent – of an individual's salary, payable when long term disability following an accident or sickness occurs. Generally speaking the policy will not make payments until 13, 26, or 52 weeks' incapacity have elapsed, but will then pay the percentage of salary until normal retirement date or until the individual returns to work.

You do not have to make new declarations for permananent health insurance; so long as the premium is paid then cover is maintained.

Life assurance

Policies are split between those which are geared specifically to provide protection for dependants and those which provide an element of such protection, but are primarly for investment purposes.

Term assurance provides a fixed sum following death during a given number of years from inception of cover, whereas family income benefit policies provide a set annual sum for a given period of years following death. A term assurance might be taken out to cover a mortgage for example, whereas a family income benefit policy is specifically geared to protect dependants.

Whole life assurance can be on a with or without profit basis and once effected will remain in force until death, provided the premiums are paid.

Endowment assurance policies provide death cover for a given number of years but accrue profits as declared by the life assurance company. At the end of the term of years, the sum assured, plus profits, is paid and this contract is often used to repay a mortgage. Unit and equity linked style contracts are now available which provide elements of life assurance plus a portion of the premium being invested in stocks, shares and property.

When arranging for protection cover always check the rates from several companies, and when looking for investment type policies check the past record of the life assurance company concerned.

Medical insurance

Private medical insurance is now available to groups and individuals. This cover enables those insured to use the services of private hospitals for treatment or operations. When proposing for this cover, always ensure that the limits you request for benefits are adequate for the hospitals in your area.

Pensions

More and more individuals are members of employers pension schemes, but if you are self-employed then you must make your own arrangements. Contributions to pension schemes are extremely tax effective and anyone who is a member of a company scheme should consider making 'additional voluntary contributions' if they are not likely to earn a maxmum pension by the time they retire.

Motor insurance

Motor insurance can be obtained from a variety of sources, and quotes should be sought from the companies direct or their agents, from motoring organisations, or from insurance brokers specialising in motor insurance, for the best bargain. All contracts of insurance are renewable annually, and therefore renegotiable.

The premium for an insurance policy will be decided on the basis of a number of facts:

(a) the past driving record, occupation and age of the driver;
(b) the type of vehicle to be driven – vehicles are divided into a number of groups for insurance purposes, depending, for example, on the engine capacity of the car and the purpose for which it is to be used;
(c) where the proposer lives – higher charges apply in large cities compared with rural areas;
(d) whether the car will be garaged at night – it is often considered to be more at risk if it is not garaged, and so the premium will be adjusted accordingly;
(e) the type of cover required.

Failure to have the necessary insurance is a very serious motoring offence, and could result in a maximum fine of up to £1,000 (the more likely fine being £125) and the collection of up to eight penalty points.

Excesses

The premium will be reduced if the insured agrees to be responsible for an excess – often the first £50 of any claim. A policy for a younger driver will normally be subject to an automatic excess. The purpose of an excess is to discourage frequent claims and to keep premiums down.

No claims bonus

Insurance companies offer a 'no claims bonus' incentive scheme, which substantially reduces the premium payable, provided that no claims have been made. The percentage reduction under the scheme goes up every year, until a maximum amount of discount is achieved, usually 60 per cent or 65 per cent.

In the event of a claim, the no claims bonus may be lost, and either you will receive no discount at the next renewal, or possibly 'step down' two levels on the insurer's discount scale. In such cases, it may be worth considering whether to pay for the damage yourself rather than claiming on your policy. A recent development has been the 'protected no claims bonus', where for an extra premium, a bonus is retained provided claims do not exceed an agreed limit.

Cover notes

A cover note acts as evidence of a valid insurance policy, and is usually issued by an insurance company as a temporary measure, to cover the vehicle and the driver for a specified period while policy documents are being drawn up.

Types of motor insurance

Third party insurance – compulsory protection for anyone you injure, including your passengers, while your car is on the public highway, whether being driven or not. In addition to the minimum legal requirement it is possible to arrange cover for damage or loss of your vehicle following fire and theft.

Fully comprehensive – will cover you for most accidents, whether or not you are at fault. It will also cover you for additional losses such as break-ins. Such insurance is obviously far more expensive than the others, and any claims will often substantially reduce the no claims bonus.

The really big drawback with fully comprehensive insurance cover, however, is that it offers no protection for the consequential losses often suffered following even a minor accident. In these cases individuals have to pursue the person at fault to recover these losses themselves at their own expense. Such losses are for obvious reasons termed 'uninsured losses' and many legal protection insurance companies offer cover to recoup them, usually through solicitors at no cost to their policyholder.

Uninsured loss recovery

A large number of possible losses and expenses related not only to the vehicle itself and personal possessions in it, but also the driver and passengers involved, may be recoverable in a legal action, as opposed to an insurance claim, for these losses. Without the insurance individuals would otherwise have to pursue the person at fault at their own cost. In no cases however does this insurance meet the loss or expense itself, only the legal cost of seeking to recover it.

Vehicle related claims may include the following:

(a) vehicle repairs or (if a write-off) replacement, if only third party fire and theft insurance exists;
(b) the claiming of a policy excess and thus the protection of a no claims bonus where the motor insurance is comprehensive;
(c) the cost of hiring alternative similar transport whilst repairs are effected;
(d) the cost of towing to a garage and possible overnight storage;
(e) the cost of temporary roadside repairs and incidental costs.

Driver/passenger related losses (such as those arising from death or personal injury) are especially important. While a comprehensive motor policy may provide limited fixed monetary payments these sums may well prove inadequate in the circumstances. With uninsured loss insurance individuals can take court action at no expense to themselves, against a negligent third party, to recover substantial damages in addition to such 'normal' payments, plus:

(a) damages for loss of contents or damage to the vehicle itself;
(b) the cost of travel home after the accident;
(c) loss of earnings.

Motor Insurers' Bureau

The Motor Insurers' Bureau provides compensation for those motorists who are involved in accidents in which the other motorist has no insurance cover. The compensation is only paid for personal injury, not damage to property. The Bureau may also assist in cases where the other vehicle does not stop following an accident, or where the owner of the other vehicle cannot be traced.

Home insurance

Structure

Having purchased a home, it is essential to insure both the building and the contents. There is no legal obligation to insure the property, but a building society or bank will insist that the buildings are covered if the purchase was financed by them. They may require you to use their services for this purpose, or they may have no objection to your making your own arrangements, but check first.

Many contracts now spread the premium over monthly instalments. Remember that the sum to be insured may be quite different (usually more) than the purchase price. This is because the actual cost of rebuilding the property may be substantially more than its current market value. Most insurance companies have an easy guide to assess the value on a square footage basis. When your property has been surveyed for mortgage purposes by the mortgagor, you will be informed of the minimum insurance value required.

Contents

Your house and its contents may be insured against various risks:

Loss or damage caused by fire, lightning, explosion, earthquake, storm, flood, theft, water or oil escaping from fixed domestic installations, landslip, subsidence or ground heave, collision by aircraft, vehicles, trains, animals, falling trees or aerials, and malicious acts; or 'all risks'.

There are three major types of policy available:

(a) *an indemnity policy* pays to restore the property or its contents to the state they were in immediately before the incident. Reductions will normally be made for wear and tear, which is why an indemnity policy is the cheapest of all policies available;

(b) a *'new-for-old'* policy makes good losses without reductions for wear and tear;

(c) *an 'all risks'* policy covers the widest range of risks, and is consequently the most expensive type of policy. Most policies usually incorporate some all risks cover for particular items, such as jewellery.

It is essential to ensure that adequate cover is taken out, and that the amount is adjusted annually to account for inflation – if you are under-insured, the percentage by which you are under-insured will be deducted from your claim. This is known as 'averaging'.

Remember: Insurers require you to cover both buildings and contents for an adequate sum. Failure to do so could result in a claim being refused or only partially paid. This is especially important where policies are issued on a 'new for old' basis where you must insure for the full replacement cost.

Occupier's liability

It is normal for a home insurance policy to include an extension to cover your liability to members of the public ('occupier's liability'; see page 61). The *buildings* policy should cover your liability as owner of the property, for example if a tile were to fall off the roof and injure a passer-by. The *contents* policy should cover your liability as occupier of the property if, for example, a visitor trips over a dangerous carpet. You should check under your contents cover to ensure that the policy includes your personal liability whilst you or your family are away from the home.

If you *employ* people to work in your home, then you should ensure that your contents policy includes cover for your liability as an employer in the event of an individual being injured whilst at work.

Holiday homes and retirement homes

When insuring a second property it is vital that you inform the insurer of the nature of the property, particularly since it may well be standing empty for considerable periods. You must disclose all material facts regarding the property and you will find that such cover is usually more expensive than for your main home. You may be required to provide additional security precautions and ensure that water is turned off when the property is unoccupied.

8.6 Contact Points

Association of British Insurers
Aldermary House
10–15 Queen Street
London EC4N 1TT
Tel: (01) 248 4477

Deals with complaints about policies issued by member companies, and offers general advice and assistance with insurance problems.

Insurance Ombudsman Bureau
31 Southampton Row
London WC1B 5HJ
Tel: (01) 242 8613

Investigates disputes between member insurance companies and their policy holders.

Personal Insurance Arbitration Service
International Arbitration Centre
75 Cannon Street
London EC4N 5BH
Tel: (01) 236 8761

Insurance Brokers Registration Council
15 St Helens Place
London EC3A 6DS
Tel: (01) 588 4387

Deals with complaints against brokers.

British Insurance Brokers Association
BIBA House
14 Bevis Marks
London EC3A 7NT
Tel: (01) 623 9043

Trade association at present representing independent insurance brokers. Acts as intermediary between individuals/brokers. Provides conciliation service. From January 1988 BIBA will be known as British Insurance and Investment Brokers Association.

Motor Insurers' Bureau
New Garden House
78 Hatton Garden
London EC1N 8JQ
Tel: (01) 242 0033

Deals with personal injury claims on behalf of victims of drivers who have no insurance, or who cannot be traced.

Glossary

Accomplice	Someone associated with another in the commission of an offence.
Accused	Someone charged with an offence.
Acquittal	Discharge from prosecution following verdict of not guilty.
Administrator	Someone appointed by the court to manage the property of a deceased person in the absence of an executor (see page 95).
Affidavit	A written statement, sworn or affirmed before, usually, a solicitor or Commissioner for Oaths.
Affiliation and Aliment	An order of the sheriff court or Court of Session declaring a person to be the father of a child and providing for the maintenance of that child (Scotland only).
Affiliation order	An order of the magistrates' court declaring a person to be the father of a child and (usually) providing for the maintenance of that child.
Aliment	Moneys agreed or ordered to be paid to a child or spouse (Scotland only)
Ancillary relief	The phrase used in divorce or separation proceedings which covers financial orders and property adjustment orders.
Appeals, civil	Appeal is said to 'lie' from a registrar to a judge in chambers; from the county court to the Court of Appeal, from the High Court to the Court of Appeal, from the Court of Appeal to the House of Lords, from the House of Lords to the European Court.

Appeals, criminal	Appeal 'lies' from the magistrates' court to the Crown Court, from the magistrates' court to Divisional Court, from the Crown Court to the Court of Appeal, from the Court of Appeal to the House of Lords, and from the House of Lords to the European Court.
Arbitration	The settling of a dispute by an arbitrator rather than in a court before a judge.
Arrest	The act of restraining and detailing a person by 'lawful authority' with or without a warrant. See page 17.
Arrestable offence	An offence for which there is a custodial (prison) sentence which is fixed by law or for which a person (not previously convicted) may be sentenced to imprisonment for a term of at least five years. An offence may be declared by statute to be arrestable although carrying a maximum period of less than five years imprisonment. See page 18.
Assault	Both a crime and a civil wrong, this is an act by which someone intentionally, or possibly recklessly, causes another to have reasonable fear of physical violence, or where actual violence has occurred.
Bail	Release of a person arrested on his giving security or accepting specific conditions. Bail will not be granted if the court believes that the defendant, if released, would fail to surrender to custody or would commit an offence while on bail. See page 25.
Battery	A crime and a civil wrong involving the actual, intended and direct use of unlawful force on a person. It includes even the slightest force; no actual harm need result.
Beneficiary	Someone who receives a gift or benefit under a will or otherwise.
Bind over	An order of a court requiring someone to agree either to do or not to do an act.
Brief	Written instructions to a barrister from a solicitor relating to legal proceedings.
Care and control	An order granting to a parent the protection, guidance and discipline of a child.

Caution	A warning used by police when it has been decided to bring prosecution. Also a form of words used when a person is arrested. See page 17.
Caveat emptor	A latin tag meaning *'let the buyer beware'*. In general the buyer is expected to look after his own interests when making a purchase. See page 27.
Citation	A document issued by the court directing someone to give evidence or to bring documents before the court (Scotland only).
Citizens' arrest	An individual's power to arrest another where an arrestable offence has been committed and he suspects, with reasonable cause, that the other is guilty of committing that offence.
Codicil	An addition or supplement to a will. It must be executed with all the formalities of an actual will. See page 94.
Committal	The act of sending someone for trial before a jury following a preliminary investigation before magistrates.
Complaint	A complaint is issued whenever information has been laid that a crime may have been committed and it has been decided to take proceedings. The complaint outlines the general nature of the offence and the place and time at which the accused is to appear in court (Scotland only).
Conditional discharge	Where the court, after finding someone guilty, and, where it considers it appropriate, discharges the offender without punishment subject to a condition that he does not commit a further offence for a specified period.
Confirmation	The order of the court which empowers the executor of a will to deal with the estate of a deceased person (Scotland only).
Consideration	Something given or accepted in return for a promise. It forms an important part of a legally enforceable contract.
Constructive dismissal	Indirect dismissal where the employee feels by the

	employer's action that there is virtually no choice but to resign. See page 134.
Contract	A legally binding agreement made either orally or in writing which usually has the three ingredients, parties price and performance. See, e.g., pages 27 and 48.
Coroner	Someone who is usually either a barrister, solicitor or registered medical practitioner of at least five years standing; conducts inquests into deaths where there is reasonable cause for suspecting violence or unnatural death. See page 91.
Counterclaim	A 'cross' action which is not a defence, which allows the defendant in the original proceedings to make a claim against the person suing him.
Credit agreement	A personal credit agreement under which the creditor provides the debtor with credit not exceeding £5,000.
Criminal Injuries Compensation Board	A government body which hears applications for payment of compensation to victims of crimes of violence. See page 149.
Curator/ix bonis	An adult through whom an infant or unwell person is entitled to sue, whose name appears on the court documents, and who undertakes to be responsible for costs. Where children are involved, depending on their age, the equivalent is a tutor/tutrix (Scotland only).
Custodianship	The vesting of the legal custody of a child in the custodian, who has fewer legal rights to the child than an adoptive parent. See page 81.
Custody of child	The actual possession of the child's person, whether or not shared with others, and not necessarily giving exclusive right to care and control.
Damages	A court's estimated compensation in money terms for a wrong suffered in contract or tort disputes.
Decree absolute	The decree which finally dissolves a marriage. Issued not earlier than six weeks from the day following the grant of the decree nisi. See page 75.
Decree nisi	A conditional decree before it is made absolute.

Defendant	Generally someone against whom legal proceedings, either civil or criminal, are bought.
Delict	A civil wrong arising from a breach of a legal duty which entitles the person owed the duty to an action of damages (Scotland only).
Dismissal (from employment)	The termination of an employee's contract of employment by the employer, with or without notice, or constructively.
Dismissal, unfair	The termination of employment contrary to employment legislation.
Dismissal, wrongful	The termination of employment without proper contractual notice.
Disqualification	The suspension of a driving licence for at least six months where 12 or more points have been collected in a three year period.
Divorce	Dissolution of marriage on the grounds of its irretrievable breakdown.
Duty of care	The duty to avoid acts or omissions which might reasonably be expected to injure another. See page 143.
Duty solicitors	Solicitors who are available on a rota basis to provide legal services in police stations and in magistrates' courts.
Employer's liability	The liability of an employer to be sued for damages by employees if they sustain personal injuries in the course of employment.
Endorsement	The recording on a driving licence of certain motoring offences, with coded particulars, indicating the type of offence which has been committed. Each endorsable offence has its own code reference and under the 'totting-up' system, endorsements totalling 12 points or more within three years brings an automatic six month driving disqualification, unless there are special circumstances. If the person who has committed the motoring offence does not possess a full driving licence, any endorsements incurred will be recorded at the DVLC and placed on the full licence when this has been obtained.

Equal pay	The legal principle that men and women doing the same or broadly similar work qualify for equal pay and conditions of employment.
Eviction	Recovering possession of land from a tenant by the landlord, eg to remove a tenant from a rented flat.
Exclusion order	A court order to exclude or dispossess a person from property to which he otherwise had a legal right (Scotland only).
Executor/ix	Someone appointed by a Will, alone or with others, to administer the testator's property and carry out provisions of the Will.
Fair dismissal	Dismissal from employment which is not contrary to employment legislation, ie on the grounds of capability, conduct, redundancy or other substantial reason, with proper notice being given.
Fair rent	Rent fixed by a rent officer under the Rent Acts after considering the age, character, locality and state of repair of the house.
Fatal accident enquiry	An enquiry into death where there is reasonable cause for suspecting violence or unnatural death, including deaths in public and deaths in hospital. The enquiry is presided over by a sheriff and will be conducted by the Procurator Fiscal (Scotland only).
'Fitness for purpose'	Where goods are sold in the course of business and the buyer makes known to the seller any particular purpose for which the goods are being bought, there is an implied condition that they are fit for that purpose.
Full committal	The act of sending someone for trial in a criminal matter before a jury following a preliminary investigation before a sheriff (Scotland only).
Grant of representation	The order of the court which empowers the executor of a Will, or the administrator where there is no Will, to deal with the estate of a deceased person.
Guarantee	A collateral contract offered when goods are sold, giving increased rights to the purchaser.

Guilty plea	Confession by the defendant that he has committed the offence with which he has been charged.
Habeas corpus	A writ used to order a person who is detaining another in custody to produce that person before the court. See page 20.
Implied agreement	Where the terms of a contract or agreement are inferred from the circumstances, or the way in which things are done or people act.
Indictment	A written or printed description of the charges laid against an accused in more serious criminal matters.
Interdict	A court order directing someone to stop doing an act complained of. Breach of the interdict is technically contempt of court and can be punished (Scotland only).
Intestacy, distribution on	The division of a deceased person's property where no vaid will exists.
Joint tenancy	The way in which two or more people hold land where on the death of one the whole estate passes to the survivor. See page 51.
Judicial separation	A decree within an existing marriage, enabling the parties to live separately.
Lump sum	A once-and-for-all cash award.
Maintenance	Financial arrangements ordered in matrimonial proceedings. See page 77.
Missives (Scotland)	Letter passing between seller's agents and purchaser's agents. Together they form the contract of sale and purchase.
Negligence	The breach of legal duty to take reasonable care or exercise reasonable skill which results in damage suffered to someone to whom the duty of care was owed. See page 143.
Next friend	An adult through whom an infant or mental patient is entitled to sue, whose name appears on the writ and undertakes to be responsible for costs.

Nuisance	Unlawful and damaging interference with another's use, enjoyment or rights in relation to land. Nuisance may be public (in which case it is also a crime) or private. See page 60.
Nullity	The description of marriages rendered void or voidable. A void marriage is one which is regarded as never having existed, whilst a voidable marriage is one that will be regarded as a valid marriage until a decree annulling it has been pronounced. See page 76.
Oath	A solemn promise (usually to God) made by witnesses in court or people 'swearing' court documents under oath before a solicitor or Commissioner for Oaths.
Occupier's liability	The 'common law' duty of care generally owed to persons lawfully on premises owned by an occupier.
Ouster injunction	A court order to exclude or dispossess a person from property to which he otherwise has a legal right.
Paramour	Generally an alleged adulterer named in divorce or judicial separation proceedings (Scotland only).
Periodical allowance	Periodic payments made by one spouse to the other, either in terms of a court order, for example following decrees of divorce or by agreement between the parties (Scotland only).
Personal representative	An administrator or executor of a deceased person.
Petition	A written application to the court which usually 'prays for relief' in various forms.
Petition (Scotland)	A petition is issued whenever information has been made available that a crime may have been committed and it has been decided to take proceedings. Petitions are used in the more serious of criminal charges; see 'Complaint' as to less serious matters. The petition outlines the general nature of the alleged offence.
Plaint	A written statement of a cause of complaint which is submitted to the court.
Plaintiff	Someone who commences an action in a civil court.
Power of attorney	A document authorising someone to act on the behalf of another. See page 89.

Product liability	The liability of manufacturer for death or personal injuries caused by a defect in products.
Pursuer	The person who initiates a civil court action in Scotland.
Quantum	The amount of money sought or payable for damages.
Rescission	The cancellation of a contract to restore the parties to their pre-contractual position.
Respondent	Someone against whom a petition is presented or an appeal is lodged.
Small claims	Claims where the amount in dispute does not exceed £500 which are heard in the county court, the procedure being simple and informal. See page 112.
Strict liability	Where a liability for damages or injury exists even though there is no negligence involved.
Subpoena	A court order directing someone to give evidence or bring documents.
Sue	The process of bringing a civil action in the courts.
Summary cause	A civil claim to the court where the amount in dispute does not exceed £1,000. These case are head in the sheriff court, and the procedure is simplified (Scotland only).
Summary offence	An offence which is triable in the magistrates' court.
Summons	A summons is issued whenever information has been laid that a crime has been committed and it has been decided to take proceedings. It states the general nature of the offence and the place and time the defendant is to appear. Also used in civil proceedings, for example to start a county court case or to apply to a registrar or judge on a point of procedure.
Surety	Someone who gives money (security) as a condition for someone being granted bail.
Tenancy in common	When two or more people hold land as tenants in common, then each has a share in it; if one dies, his share does not pass to the other automatically.

Third party	Someone other than the two main parties involved in court proceedings.
Tort	A civil wrong arising from a breach of a legal duty which entitles the person owed the duty of care to an action for damages, eg negligence – see page 58.
Trespass	An unlawful interference with a person's land or possessions.
Ward of court	A child who has been placed under the care of a guardian appointed by the court.
Warrant	A document issued by the magistrates' court ordering someone to be brought before the court.
Warranty	An agreement which is connected with a contract of sale, the breach of which gives rise to a claim for damages.
Writ	A document issued by a higher court to commence a court action.

INDEX

ACAS (Advisory, Conciliation and
    Arbitration Service)   137–138, 140
ALAS (Accident Legal Advice Service)   9
Abduction of child   78–79
Abortion   80
Abroad, travelling   35–36, 120–122
Access to children   78
Accident   36, 39, 143–149
    failing to stop after   39
    road   36, 39, 146
    school, at   148
    sporting   149
    work, at   146–148
Accommodation agency   55
Act of God   143
Action for Victims of Medical
    Accidents   104, 150
Adoption   80–81
Advertising   120
Advertising Standards Authority   120, 125
Advisory Centre for Education   100
Advisory Conciliation and Arbitration
    Service (ACAS)   137–138, 140
Advocates   9
Affiliation   72
Age concern   106
Age-limits   34–35, 83–85, 122
Agreement for tenancy   52
Alcohol
    see Drink and driving; Licensing laws
Aliment   72
Animals   59, 60, 86
Annulment of marriage   76–77
Arbitration   112
Architects Registration Council   61
Arrest, power of   17–18
Association of British Insurers   158
Association of British Laundry,
    Cleaning and Rental Services   126

Association of British Travel Agents
    (ABTA)   120, 128
Association of Carers   105
Association of Mail Order Publishers   111
Attorney, power of   89–90
Attorney-General   3
Auction sales   31, 110
Automobile Association   44

Bail   25
Bank   114–115
Bank loan   57, 117
    see also Credit; Financing
Banking Ombudsman   126
Barristers   3, 9
Battered wives   73–74
Bigamy   72
Birth   79
Blood sample in drink/drive case   43
Breach of the peace   18
Breath testing   41–42
Breathalyser   41–42
Brick Development Association   63
British Agencies for Adoption and
    Fostering   102
British Association for Counselling   98
British Association of Removers   66
British Chemical Dampcourse
    Association   65
British Decorators Association   66
British Insurance Brokers Association   159
British Medical Association   105
British Telecom Users' Association   127
British Wood Preserving Association   65
Buggery   86
Building Research Establishment   63
Building Societies Ombudsman   64–65
Building regulations   57–58
Building society loan   57, 117

Building works   56–58
Buildings insurance   157, 158
Buying a car   27–31
Buying goods and services   107–109

Car
    see Motor vehicle
Careless driving   39
Case-law   1
Causing death by reckless driving   39
Caution given by police   17, 19
'Caveat emptor'   27, 29
'Chains' in conveyancing   48
Chancery Division   3
Charge, criminal   15
Chartered Institute of Arbitrators 112, 128
Cheque(s)   114–115
Child Poverty Action Group   97
Child
    abduction of   78–79
    abuse   85–86
    access to   78
    adoption of   80–81
    arrangements for on divorce   74, 75, 76
    crime by   83
    custodianship of   81
    custody of   78
    fostering of   81
    illegitimate   80
    maintenance of   77
    obligations of parent to   82
    protection of   60, 61, 85–86
    resonsibility of parent for   82
    safety of   60, 61, 148
    school, at   148
    wardship of   82
'Childline'   96
Childrens' Legal Centre   100
Church-marriages   70–71
Circuit judges   3
Civil marriage   71
Closed shop   137
Cohabitation   72–73
Commission for Racial Equality   139
Common land   59
Complaint
    medical treatment, about   88
    goods purchase, about   111–113
    motor vehicle, about   29, 33
    police, against   22–23

Completion of contract to purchase
    home   49
Conciliation   77–78
Conditional sale agreement   31
Constructive dismissal   134
Consumer Consultative Council   113
Consumer affairs   107–128
Consumers Association   124
Contents insurance   157–158
Contraception   80
Contract
    child, made by   82–83
    employment, of   129–132
    sale, for   107–108
    sale/purchase of home, for   48–49
Contributory negligence   145
Conveyancing   47–50
Coroner   91–92
Cost of conveyancing   49–50
Council of Licensed Conveyancers   48, 62
Countryside Commission   64
Court, consumer complaint in   112–113
Court of Protection   89, 103
Court of Session   4
Courts   1–8
Credit   115–117
    see also Bank loan; Financing
Credit cards   115
Credit sale agreement   31, 116–117
Criminal Injuries Compensation Board   149
Criminal proceedings, legal aid for   13–14
Crown Court   3
Crown Prosecution Service   25
Custodianship   81
Custody of children   78
Customs and Excise   122

Damp treatment   51
Dangerous animal   86
Dealer
    buying car from   27–29
Death   90–92
    presumption of   78
    without having made a will   93–94
Delict   58
Department of Transport   45
Deposits   110
Detention by police   18–19
Direct Selling Association   125
Disability Alliance   106

Discipline at work 133
Discrimination 136
Dismissal from employment 133–135
  see also Redundancy
Disqualification from driving 38, 39–43
District Court 4
Divorce 74–76, 94
  procedure 75–76
Domestic violence 73–74
Doorstep sales 110
Drink and driving 40–43
Driver and Vehicle Licensing Centre
  (DVLC) 45
Driving Licence 34, 35, 39
'Drugline' 100
Drugs
  driving and 42
  liability of manufacturer for
    safety of 119
Duty solicitors 22

EEC law 1–2
  decisions 2
  Directives 2
  Regulations 2
Education 82
Education Otherwise 101
Electricity Consumers Council 127
Employment law 129–141
Engagement to be married 69
Entry, power of 20
Environmental Health Department 113, 125
Equal Opportunities Commission 139
Equal pay 136
Equal Pay and Opportunity Campaign 140
Estimate for repairs 32–33
European Community law 1–2
Ex-spouse, maintenance of 77
Exclusion clauses 108, 109
External Wall Insulation Association 65
Eyesight, defective, driving with 40

Fair rent 54
Families Need Fathers 99
Family Division of the High Court 3
Family Practitioner Committee 88
Family Rights Group 101
Federation of Master Builders 58, 63

Financing
  home improvements 56–57
  purchase of motor vehicle 30–31
  see also Bank
Fire Protection Association 150
Firearms 123–124
Fixed penalties 37–38
Flat
  see Home
Food 118–119
Fostering 81
Funerals 92

Gas Consumer Council 127
General Dental Council 105
General Medical Council 105
General practitioner
  complaints against 88
General Register Office 104
Gingerbread 99
Glass and Glazing Federation 66
Glossary of terms 161 et seq
Goods, safety of 117–119
Grants for home improvements 56
'Green card' 35
Green form 10–11
Guns 123–124

Habeas corpus 20
Health
  see Medical
Health Service Commissioner
  (Ombudsman) 104
Health and Safety Executive 140–141
Health and safety at work 138–139
Heating and Ventilation Contractors
  Association 65
High Court Judges 3
High Court of Justiciary 4
Hire Purchase 116–117
Holiday home 158
Holidays 120–122
  see also Travelling abroad
Home 47–67
  accidents in 148–149
  buying and selling 47–50
  damp and timber treatment 51
  guarantees 50
  improvements 56–58
  insurance 56, 157–158

Home (contd)
jointly owned	51
moving	61
offences relating to	58–61
Hospitals	87–88
Hours of work	131
House	
see Home	
House of Lords	2, 3
Human remains	92
Illegitimacy	80
Imprisonment	19–20
Incest	86
Incest Crisis Line	96–97
Incorporated Association of	
Architects	62
Incorporated Society of Valuers and	
Auctioneers	64
Independent Broadcasting Authority	125
Independent Schools Information	
Service	101
Industrial	
injury	146–148
relations	137–138
safety	138–139
tribunal	134–135, 140
Inheritance tax	96
Injunction	58, 60, 73–74
Inland Revenue Stamp Duty Office	106
Inquest	91–92
Institute for Study of Drug	
Dependence	100
Insurance	151–159
broker	151–152
Brokers Registration Council	152, 159
claim	152
home, of	56, 157–158
legal expenses	14–15
motor	154–156
Ombudsman	159
Interdict	58, 73–74
International Motor Insurance Card	
(green card)	35
Intestacy	95
Joint ownership of home	51
Judiciary	2–4
Justice for Children	100
Juvenile crime	83

King's Counsel	3
Landlord, responsibilities of	53
Law Society, The	26, 50
Law Society of Northern Ireland	26
Law Society of Scotland	26
Learner driver	35
Legal advice, right to when detained	22
Legal advice and assistance	11–12
Legal aid	9, 10–14
civil	12–13
criminal	13–14
Legal Aid Board (Scotland)	26
Legal expenses insurance	14–15
Legal profession	9–10
Letting a home	54–55
Licensed conveyancers	50
Licensing laws	122–123
Life assurance	153–154
Loan	
see Bank loan, Financing, Overdraft	
Lord Chancellor	2
Lord Chief Justice	3, 4
Lords Justices of Appeal	3
Lords of Appeal	2–3
MOT certificate	34, 36
Magistrates	3–4
Mail order	111
Mail Order Protection Scheme	126
Mail Order Traders' Association	111, 126
Maintenance of parties to marriage	71, 74
Marital rights and obligations	71
Marriage	69–72
annulment of	76–77
effect of on a will	94
termination of	74–79
Marriage Guidance Council	102
Master of the Rolls	3
Maternity rights	132–133
Matrimonial property	73
Meals in restaurants	119–120
Medical	
Victims Association	150
insurance	154
treatment, consent to	87
Mental health	89–90
Merchantable quality	27, 32, 107
MIND	103
Misrepresentation	27, 29, 32, 48, 109

Missive 48
Mortgage 47, 49, 57, 71
Motor Agents Association Ltd 28, 43
Motor
  abroad 35–36
  conditional sale agreement 31
  credit sale agreement 31
  dealer 27–28
  documentation required for 33–34
  hire of 36
  hire purchase 30–31
  insurance 34, 36, 37, 40, 154–156
  Insurers Bureau 156, 159
  maintenance of 38–39
  MOT certificate 34
  offences in connection with 36, 37–43
  parking 37
  purchasing 27–31
  repairs to and servicing 32–33
  selling 31–32
  stopping and searching 17
  tax disc 34
  vehicle 27–45
Moving house 61

NSPCC 97
National Association for the Welfare
  of Children in Hospital 99
National Association of
  Conveyancers 50, 62
National Association of Estate Agents 64
National Association of Funeral
  Directors 92, 106
National Association of Young People's
  Counselling Advisory Services 98
National Association of Young People
  in Care 102
National Cavity Insulation Association 65
National Childrens Bureau 98
National Consumer Council 124
National Council for Civil Liberties 25
National Council for One Parent
  Families 99
National Family Conciliation Council
  77, 102
National Foster Care Association 100
National Health Service 87–88
National House-Building Council 50, 63
National Society for the Prevention of
  Cruelty to Children (NSPCC) 97

National Step Family Association 101
Negligence 85, 88, 109, 143–145
No claims bonus 155
Noise 60
Noise Abatement Society 67
Northern Ireland Association for
  Mental Health 104
Notice to quit 55–56, 73
Notice to terminate employment 130
Nuisance 60–61

Occupier's liability 61, 158
Off licence 122
Office of Fair Trading 120, 124
Office of the Wages Council 140
OFGAS 127
OFTEL 127
Ombudsman 113
Organization for Parents under Stress 97
Overdraft 114, 117

PAIN 106
Parent to Parent Information on
  Adoption 103
Parent, obligations of 82
Parents for Children 103
Parking of cars 37
Patients Association 150
Pay 130–131, 136
  see also Maternity rights
Penalties for road traffic offences 38–43
Penalty points 38–43
Pensions 154
Permanent health insurance 153
Personal Insurance Arbitration Service 159
Personal accident insurance 153
Personal representatives 92, 94–96
Personal search 21–22
Planning permisson 57–58
Police 15–23
  hierarchy 15–16
  powers 16–22
Police Complaints Authority 23, 26
Police Station
  legal advice and assistance at 22
Polygamy 72
Post Office Users National Council 128
Post mortem 90–91
Post, buying by 111
Power of arrest 17–18

Power of attorney 89–90
'Precedents' 1
Pregnancy 132–133
Premises, powers of police to enter
and search 20–21
Prison sentences 23–24
Probate 93–96
Procurator Fiscal 91
Product liability 119
Prosecution 25
Public houses 122–123
Purchasing
goods and services 107–109
motor vehicle 27–31

Queen's Bench Division 3
Queen's Counsel 3
Quotation for repairs 32–33

Radio Electrical and Television
Retailers Association 126
Rape Crisis Centre 98
Rape Crisis Line 98
Re-employment, right of in maternity
case 132–133
Reckless driving 39
Redundancy 135–136
Registration of birth 79
Registration of death 90
Register office, marriage in 71
Removals 61
Rent Acts 51–52
Rent book 53, 55
Renting a home 51–56, 73
Repairs to motor vehicle 32–33
Resident magistrate 4
Restaurants 119–120
Retirement home 55, 158
Rights of way 59–60
Road accident 36, 146
Road fund licence 34
Road traffic law 27–45
Roadworthy condition 29, 38
Royal Automobile Club 44
Royal Institute of British Architects 62
Royal Institute of Chartered Surveyors 64
Royal Scottish Society for the Prevention
of Cruelty to Children 97
Royal Society for the Prevention of
Accidents 150

Safety at work 130, 138–139, 146–148
Safety of goods 117–119
School, accidents at 148
Scottish Adoption Advice Centre 103
Scottish Association for Mental Health 103
Scottish Family Conciliation Council 102
Scottish Motor Trade Association 44
Search, powers of police to 16–17, 20–22
Search warrant 20–21
Seat belts 37, 38, 145
Sentencing 23
Separation, judicial 76
Service charges in restaurants 119–120
Servicing motor vehicle 32–34
Sheriff Principal 4
Sheriff court 4
Shorthold tenancy 53–54
Shotgun 123
Sick pay 131
Sickness insurance 153
Small Claims Court 112–113
Society of Motor Manufacturers and
Traders 44
Solicitor General 3
Solicitors 8
Solicitors Complaints Bureau 26, 50
Solicitors Family Law Association 101
Somerset House 104
Sources of law 1
Speeding 40
Sporting accidents 149
Squatters 60, 148
Statutes 1
Statutory sick pay 131
Step Family Association 101
Stipendiary magistrates 3
Stop and search powers of police 16–23
'Strict liability' 145
Sub-letting 55
Summary cause court 112
Surveyor 47

Tax disc 34
Tenancy agreements 52
Tenancy of home 51–56, 73
Tenant, responsibilities of 53
Thalidomide 119
Timber treatment 51
Time-limits
negligence claims 145

Tort	58	Vice Chancellor	3
Trade unions	137		
Trading Standards Office	113, 118, 125	Wages	130–131, 136
Travel agent	120	Wages Councils	138
Travelling abroad	35–36, 120–122	Wardship	82
Trespass	58–59	Warrant for arrest	18
		Wedding presents	69
Unfair contract terms	109	Wild flowers	59–60
Unfair dismissal		Wills	93–96
see Dismissal from employment		Work	
'Uninsured loss recovery'	156	*see* Employment law	
Unsolicited goods and services	110	Work, accidents at	146–148
		Wrongful dismissal	136
Vehicle Builders and Repairers			
Association	44	Youth custody	24